Low-Fat Italian Cookbook

By the Editors of Sunset Books

Sunset Publishing Corporation • Menlo Park, CA

Sunset
BOOKS

President & Publisher
Susan J. Maruyama

Director, Sales & Marketing
Richard A. Smeby

Director, New Business
Kenneth Winchester

Editorial Director
Bob Doyle

Production Director
Lory Day

•

**EDITORIAL STAFF FOR
LOW-FAT ITALIAN**

Developmental Editor
Linda J. Selden

Research & Text
Karyn I. Lipman

Copy Editor
Rebecca LaBrum

Design
Susan Sempere

Illustrations
Dick Cole

Dietary Consultant
Patricia Kearney, R.D.
Stanford University Hospital

Photo Stylist
Sandra Griswold

Food Stylist
Heidi Gintner

Assistant Food & Photo Stylist
Elizabeth C. Davis

Photographer
Allan Rosenberg

Associate Photographer
Allen V. Lott

Production Coordinator
Patricia S. Williams

•

**SUNSET PUBLISHING
CORPORATION**

Chairman
Jim Nelson

President & Chief Executive Officer
Stephen J. Seabolt

Chief Financial Officer
James E. Mitchell

Publisher, Sunset Magazine
Anthony P. Glaves

Director of Finance
Larry Diamond

Circulation Director
Robert I. Gursha

Vice President, Manufacturing
Lorinda B. Reichert

Editor, Sunset Magazine
William R. Marken

A Low-fat Feast of Italian Extraction

Think of Italian food: fresh, bright, vividly seasoned, full of tantalizing flavors and aromas. Now think of low-fat Italian food—and the description needn't change at all. As this new book will demonstrate, dining Italian-style and cooking lean are not mutually exclusive. Enjoy classics like lasagne, linguine with clam sauce, focaccia, creamy risotto, and luscious tiramisu; or try less traditional choices, such as beef tenderloin with cherry-wine sauce or vegetarian sandwiches filled with portabella mushrooms.

The recipes in this book conform to the American Heart Association's recommendations for fat intake; in each, fat accounts for no more than 30% of the total calories. Every recipe is accompanied by a nutritional analysis (see page 5) prepared by Hill Nutrition Associates, Inc., of Florida. We are grateful to Lynne Hill, R.D., for her advice and expertise.

Each recipe also lists preparation and cooking times. Keep in mind that these times are approximate and will vary depending on your expertise in the kitchen and the cooking equipment you use.

The recipes in this book were developed in the Sunset Test Kitchens. If you have comments or suggestions, please let us hear from you. Write to us at:

**Sunset Books / Cookbook Editorial
80 Willow Road
Menlo Park, CA 94025**

First printing June 1996
Copyright © 1996 Sunset Publishing Corporation,
Menlo Park, CA 94025. First edition. All rights reserved, including the right of reproduction in whole or in any form.
ISBN 0-376-02485-2
Library of Congress Catalog Card: 95-072209
Printed in the United States.

If you would like to order additional copies of any of our books,
call us at 1 800 634-3095 or check with your local bookstore.
For special sales, bulk orders, and premium sales information,
call Sunset Custom Publishing & Special Sales at (415) 324-5547.

Front cover: *Fettuccine Alfredo (recipe on page 71). Design by Susan Bryant Caron. Photography by Allan Rosenberg. Photo styling by Sandra Griswold. Food styling by Heidi Gintner.*

Contents

Roasted Garlic (recipe on page 36)

Special Features

Buon Appetito!

Farm-fresh vegetables and fruits, splendidly seasoned sauces, pasta in every shape and size, satisfying polenta and risotto—all these are characteristic of Italian cooking. And all are well-suited for lean meals. In fact, dining Italian style and cutting fat are so compatible that you can enjoy many favorite dishes with remarkably little alteration—sometimes, none at all. A suppertime standard such as tender-firm linguine or sturdy polenta topped with a brilliant combination of Roma tomatoes, sweet peppers, garlic, and zippy fresh basil (see page 17) would earn any nutritionist's blessing. When you do need to alter the classic recipes, it may be enough just to decrease the quantity of oil or butter, reduce the cheese from a shower to a light sprinkle, or adjust your favorite pasta dishes to include a little more pasta and a little less sauce.

A look through this book will show you how simple it is to prepare lean dishes with authentic Italian flavor. Take focaccia (pages 60–61), for example. The traditional bread base is already low in fat, so all you need to do is devise a similarly streamlined topping. That means going easy on the cheese and meat, opting instead for lots of vegetables (or even fruits). Risotto (see page 15) is another easily slimmed-down classic. The traditional slow simmering of rice in broth captures the creamy-rich texture of the original, and the lavish addition of vegetables such as mushrooms and pungent greens lends so much appeal you won't miss the butter and cheese we've left out. Even an all-time favorite like Eggplant Parmesan (page 66) can suit a light menu nicely. We baked the crumb-coated eggplant slices instead of frying them, cut down on the mozzarella cheese, and added lots of flavor with a double dose of tomatoes—sliced ripe ones in the casserole, plus a zesty herb-and-garlic tomato sauce to bind all the ingredients together.

Italian-style desserts, too, can be perfect for low-fat meals. As always, start by choosing those that are already lean: intensely flavored ices (pages 87 and 88), crunchy biscotti (pages 84–85), and dense, fruity Panforte (page 90) come to mind. But even emphatically luxurious treats such as Tiramisu (page 80) don't have to remain out of reach in high-fat heaven. Our version uses the classic brandy-soaked ladyfingers as the base, but lightens up the filling by cutting down on the super-rich mascarpone and supplementing it with non-fat cream cheese and whipped topping. The result, though fluffier than genuine *tiramisù*, provides just as luscious a "pick-me-up" with a hot cup of espresso.

Shopping for Ingredients

If you buy the foods you normally would for Italian cooking, you've already stocked up on much of what you need for low-fat Italian meals: poultry, lean meats, and seafood, the best produce, pasta (both fresh and dried), short- or medium-grain rice, polenta, olive oil, Parmesan and mozzarella cheeses, and canned goods such as tomatoes, garbanzos, and cannellini beans. You may want to pay extra attention to seasonings and condiments, though, since adding more flavor is a great way to make up for using less fat. Fresh herbs, aromatic balsamic and wine vinegars, and pungent spices and seeds really make simple dishes sing. Other flavor-boosters include rich, tangy dried tomatoes, silky roasted peppers, and sweet oven-roasted garlic (see pages 36–37). Olives, delicate toasted pine nuts, and fragrant pesto sauces (see page 68) make marvelous accents too—but since these are high in fat, be sure you use them sparingly.

When a recipe calls for dairy products, we typically specify nonfat, low-fat, or reduced-fat choices. Among cheeses, we also favor modest amounts of whole-milk types such as Gorgonzola, provolone, fontina, and Parmesan; these are all so assertive that a small amount makes a significant contribution to a recipe's flavor. Another favorite is smoked mozzarella; stronger tasting than the plain cheese, it lends a wonderful savor to dishes such as Pasta & Cheese Pie (page 24).

An easy way to decrease the percentage of calories from fat in any meal is to include pasta, rice, or polenta on the menu. Where Italian cooking is concerned, of course, this tactic almost goes without saying, since so many dishes are based on pasta. But think about combinations beyond the familiar pair of pasta-and-sauce: serve grilled lamb chops with polenta, for example (see page 55), or present broiled chicken breasts on a bed of flavorful risotto.

Cooking Techniques

Baking, broiling, grilling, and steaming are the standard low-fat cooking methods, and all are represented in this book. Many of our recipes also feature braise-deglazing, a lean version of sautéing used to develop a flavorful base of cooked onions or other vegetables for a variety of dishes. To braise-deglaze, you simply omit some or all of the fat you'd typically use for pan-frying, instead adding a little water or broth to the vegetables you want to cook. Stir the mixture over medium-high to medium heat until the vegetables begin to brown and the liquid is gone; then stir in a bit more liquid, gently scraping free any browned bits sticking to the pan bottom. Repeat the process until the vegetables are as soft and browned as you like. Although braise-deglazing doesn't brown foods as quickly as sautéing

does, you'll find that vegetables cooked in this way have every bit as much deep, rich flavor and color as those cooked in fat.

Using Our Recipes

When you follow our recipes, you may want to make substitutions to achieve the flavor you like. In some cases, you may decide to use products higher in fat or sodium than those we specify; perhaps you prefer part-skim ricotta cheese to the nonfat version, or regular canned broth to the reduced-sodium type. Just be aware that such substitutions will boost the fat or sodium content of the finished dish.

Another point to consider is that low-fat does not always mean low-calorie. If you're trying to lose weight on a calorie-controlled diet, be aware of your daily limit and select foods accordingly. Many of the recipes in this book will fit right into your plan, but some are high enough in calories to qualify as occasional treats.

Remember that the preparation and cooking times given in our recipes are guides, not absolutes. Actual times will vary, depending on your level of expertise, the type of heat source and cookware you have, the ripeness or firmness of the fruits and vegetables you use, and so on.

A Word About Our Nutritional Data

For our recipes, we provide a nutritional analysis stating calorie count; percentage of calories from fat; grams of total fat and saturated fat; milligrams of cholesterol and sodium; grams of carbohydrates, fiber, and protein; and milligrams of calcium and iron. Generally, the analysis applies to a single serving, based on the number of servings given for each recipe and the amount of each ingredient. If a range is given for the number of servings and/or the amount of an ingredient, the analysis is based on the average of the figures given.

The nutritional analysis does not include optional ingredients or those for which no specific amount is stated. If an ingredient is listed with a substitution, the information was calculated using the first choice.

Baked Fennel with Gorgonzola
(recipe on page 8)

Side Dishes

Fresh, nutritious vegetables and fruits play a big part in any low-fat diet, and lean Italian cuisine is no exception. Accompaniments such as Roasted Vegetable Medley, Poached Leeks with Hazelnuts, and elegant Fruited Spinach Purée offer delicious, colorful ways to dress up and round out the simplest of meals. Of course, favorite Italian side dishes include more than just vegetable specialties. You'll find pasta and polenta in this chapter too, from hot, hearty choices like Polenta with Fresh Tomato Sauce to cool salads such as Pastina with Peas.

Baked Fennel with Gorgonzola

Braised fresh fennel with a baked-on blue cheese topping is a nice accompaniment for your favorite fish fillets or steaks.

Preparation time: 15 minutes
Cooking time: About 50 minutes
Pictured on page 6

½ cup (50 g) fine dry bread crumbs

4 large heads fennel (about 3 lbs./1.35 kg *total*)

1¾ cups (420 ml) fat-free reduced-sodium chicken broth

3 tablespoons packed crumbled Gorgonzola, cambozola, or other blue-veined cheese
Salt and pepper

1. Sprinkle three-fourths of the bread crumbs over bottom of a rectangular baking dish (about 8 by 12 inches/20 by 30 cm). Set aside.

2. Trim stems from fennel, reserving about 1 cup (30 g) of the feathery green leaves. Trim and discard any bruised areas from fennel; then cut each fennel head in half lengthwise. Lay fennel halves in a wide frying pan. Pour broth into pan and bring to a boil over high heat; then reduce heat, cover, and simmer until fennel is tender when pierced (about 25 minutes). With a slotted spoon, transfer fennel halves to baking dish, arranging them in a single layer with cut side up.

3. Bring cooking broth to a boil over high heat; boil until reduced to ½ cup (120 ml), about 10 minutes. Stir in half the reserved fennel leaves. Spoon mixture over fennel halves in baking dish.

4. In a small bowl, mash cheese with remaining bread crumbs and 1 teaspoon water; dot mixture evenly over fennel. Bake in a 375°F (190°C) oven until topping begins to brown and fennel is heated through (about 15 minutes). Tuck remaining fennel leaves around fennel halves. Season to taste with salt and pepper. Makes 8 servings.

Per serving: 74 calories (28% calories from fat), 2 g total fat, 1 g saturated fat, 5 mg cholesterol, 416 mg sodium, 9 g carbohydrates, 2 g fiber, 4 g protein, 113 mg calcium, 2 mg iron

Baked Zucchini with Mushrooms

Delicious with roast pork, this hearty casserole will remind you of an oven-baked frittata.

Preparation time: 20 minutes
Cooking time: About 1 hour

1 pound (455 g) mushrooms, thinly sliced

1 medium-size onion, chopped
About 1⅓ cups (320 ml) canned vegetable broth

3 large eggs

4 large zucchini (about 2 lbs./905 g *total*), shredded

½ cup (50 g) fine dry bread crumbs

¼ cup (20 g) grated Parmesan cheese

¼ teaspoon *each* pepper and dried oregano

2 tablespoons thinly sliced green onion

1. In a wide nonstick frying pan, combine mushrooms, chopped onion, and ½ cup (120 ml) water. Cook over medium-high heat, stirring often, until liquid has evaporated and vegetables are beginning to brown. To deglaze, add ⅓ cup (80 ml) of the broth and stir to scrape browned bits free from pan bottom. Then continue to cook, stirring occasionally, until vegetables begin to brown again. Repeat deglazing and browning steps 2 or 3 more times, using ⅓ cup (80 ml) broth each time; onion should be golden brown (about 15 minutes *total*). Remove pan from heat.

2. In a large bowl, beat eggs to blend; stir in mushroom mixture, zucchini, bread crumbs, cheese, pepper, and oregano.

3. Pour egg mixture into a greased 9- by 13-inch (23- by 33-cm) baking dish; spread out evenly. Bake in a 325°F (165°C) oven until casserole appears set in center when dish is gently shaken (about 45 minutes). Let stand for 5 to 10 minutes; then sprinkle with green onion and serve. Makes 8 servings.

Per serving: 112 calories (30% calories from fat), 4 g total fat, 1 g saturated fat, 82 mg cholesterol, 306 mg sodium, 14 g carbohydrates, 2 g fiber, 7 g protein, 85 mg calcium, 2 mg iron

Sautéed mushrooms laced with sherry and balsamic vinegar embellish these tender-crisp green beans.

- 1 tablespoon butter or margarine
- 1 small onion, finely chopped
- 1 pound (455 g) mushrooms, finely chopped
- ½ cup (120 ml) dry sherry
- 1 tablespoon (15 ml) reduced-sodium soy sauce
- 2 tablespoons (30 ml) balsamic vinegar
- 1 teaspoon *each* cornstarch and Oriental sesame oil
- 3 pounds (1.35 kg) green beans, ends trimmed

Green Beans with Sautéed Mushrooms

Preparation time: 20 minutes
Cooking time: About 30 minutes

1. Melt butter in a wide nonstick frying pan over medium-high heat. Add onion and cook, stirring often, until soft. Add mushrooms, ¼ cup (60 ml) of the sherry, and ¼ cup (60 ml) water; cook, stirring often, until almost all liquid has evaporated and mushrooms are lightly browned (about 15 minutes).

2. In a small bowl, stir together remaining ¼ cup (60 ml) sherry, ½ cup (120 ml) water, soy sauce, vinegar, cornstarch, and oil. Add to mushroom mixture and cook, stirring, until sauce boils and thickens slightly. Remove from heat and keep warm.

3. In a 5- to 6-quart (5- to 6-liter) pan, bring 3 quarts (2.8 liters) water to a boil over high heat. Add beans; cook, uncovered, until just tender to bite (4 to 6 minutes). Drain well, arrange on a platter, and top with mushroom-onion mixture. Makes 12 servings.

Per serving: 70 calories (21% calories from fat), 2 g total fat, 0.7 g saturated fat, 3 mg cholesterol, 69 mg sodium, 10 g carbohydrates, 2 g fiber, 3 g protein, 42 mg calcium, 2 mg iron

---

A lemon-sherry vinaigrette flavors fennel, green beans, and chunks of russet potato in a dish that's just right for a buffet.

- 2 large heads fennel (about 1½ lbs./680 g *total*)
- 1 pound (455 g) slender green beans, ends trimmed
- 2 tablespoons (30 ml) olive oil
- 2 very large russet potatoes (about 1½ lbs./680 g *total*), peeled and cut into 1-inch (2.5-cm) chunks
- 1 teaspoon *each* mustard seeds, cumin seeds, and fennel seeds
- ⅓ cup (80 ml) sherry vinegar
- ⅓ cup (80 ml) Gewürztraminer or orange juice
- 1 tablespoon grated lemon peel

1. Trim stems from fennel, reserving some of the feathery green leaves

Roasted Potatoes, Fennel & Green Beans with Sherry Dressing

Preparation time: 25 minutes
Cooking time: 50 to 60 minutes

for garnish. Trim and discard any bruised areas from fennel; then cut fennel into ¾-inch (2-cm) chunks. Transfer to a large, shallow baking pan. Add beans and 4 teaspoons (20 ml) of the oil; stir to coat vegetables. In a 9-inch-square (23-cm-square) baking pan, mix potatoes and remaining 2 teaspoons oil.

2. Bake all vegetables in a 475°F (245°C) oven, stirring occasionally,

until richly browned (about 45 minutes for fennel and beans, 50 to 60 minutes for potatoes). Watch carefully to prevent scorching. As pieces brown, remove them and keep warm; add water, ¼ cup (60 ml) at a time, if pans appear dry.

3. While vegetables are baking, stir mustard seeds, cumin seeds, and fennel seeds in a small frying pan over medium heat until fragrant (2 to 5 minutes). Remove pan from heat and stir in vinegar, Gewürztraminer, and lemon peel; set aside.

4. Transfer fennel, beans, and potatoes to a large rimmed serving bowl; add dressing and mix gently to coat vegetables. Garnish with reserved fennel leaves. Makes 4 to 6 servings.

Per serving: 210 calories (27% calories from fat), 6 g total fat, 0.7 g saturated fat, 0 mg cholesterol, 126 mg sodium, 33 g carbohydrates, 5 g fiber, 5 g protein, 99 g calcium, 3 mg iron

Crisp pine nuts top this colorful combination of chard, red bell pepper, and currants.

Sautéed Chard with Pine Nuts

Preparation time: 15 minutes
Cooking time: About 10 minutes

1½ pounds (680 g) Swiss chard
1 tablespoon pine nuts
1 teaspoon olive oil
2 cloves garlic, minced or pressed
1 large red bell pepper (about 8 oz./230 g), seeded and cut into slivers about 2 inches (5 cm) long
⅓ cup (50 g) dried currants

1. Cut off and discard coarse stem ends of chard. Rinse and drain chard. Then thinly slice stems crosswise up to base of leaves; set sliced stems aside. Use a few whole leaves to line a large rimmed serving dish; coarsely chop remaining leaves. Set aside serving dish and all chard.

2. Toast pine nuts in a wide nonstick frying pan over medium heat until golden (about 3 minutes), stirring often. Pour out of pan and set aside. Heat oil in pan over medium-high heat. Add garlic, chard stems, and 1 tablespoon (15 ml) water; cook, stirring, until stems are softened (about 2 minutes). Stir in chopped leaves, bell pepper, and currants. Cover and cook until leaves are wilted (about 5 minutes), stirring occasionally.

3. With a slotted spoon, lift chard mixture from pan and arrange in serving dish. Sprinkle with pine nuts. Makes 4 servings.

Per serving: 105 calories (20% calories from fat), 3 g total fat, 0.3 g saturated fat, 0 mg cholesterol, 336 mg sodium, 20 g carbohydrates, 2 g fiber, 4 g protein, 99 mg calcium, 4 mg iron

---

A zesty vinaigrette dresses up these tender whole artichokes.

Roasted Artichokes with Vinaigrette

Preparation time: 30 minutes
Cooking time: About 1¼ hours
Chilling time: At least 2 hours
Pictured on facing page

4 large artichokes (*each* 4 to 4½ inches/10 to 11 cm in diameter)
2 cups (470 ml) fat-free reduced-sodium chicken broth
1 teaspoon *each* dried rosemary, dried oregano, dried thyme, and mustard seeds
¼ cup (60 ml) balsamic vinegar
1 pound (455 g) pear-shaped (Roma-type) tomatoes, seeded and chopped
⅓ cup (35 g) sliced green onions
2 tablespoons chopped Italian or regular parsley

1. Break small, coarse outer leaves from artichokes. With a sharp knife, cut off thorny tops; with scissors, snip any remaining thorny tips from leaves. With knife, peel stems and trim bases. Immerse artichokes in water and swish up and down to rinse well; lift out and, holding by stem end, shake to remove water.

2. Place artichokes in a 9- by 13-inch (23- by 33-cm) baking pan. Mix broth, 1 cup (240 ml) water, rosemary, oregano, thyme, and mustard seeds; pour into pan. Cover very tightly with foil and bake in a 450°F (230°C) oven until artichoke bottoms are tender when pierced (about 50 minutes). Uncover and continue to bake until artichokes are just tinged with brown (about 8 more minutes).

3. With a slotted spoon, lift artichokes from pan. Hold briefly above pan to drain; transfer to a rimmed dish. Reserve juices in pan. When artichokes are cool enough to touch, ease center of each open; using a spoon, scoop out a few of the tiny center leaves and the choke.

4. Boil pan juices over high heat until reduced to ½ cup (120 ml), about 10 minutes. Remove from heat, stir in vinegar, and pour over artichokes. Cover; refrigerate for at least 2 hours or until next day, spooning marinade over artichokes occasionally.

5. With a slotted spoon, transfer artichokes to individual plates. Stir tomatoes, onions, and parsley into artichoke marinade; spoon mixture around artichokes and into their centers. Makes 4 servings.

Per serving: 96 calories (7% calories from fat), 0.9 g total fat, 0.1 g saturated fat, 0 mg cholesterol, 441 mg sodium, 19 g carbohydrates, 8 g fiber, 7 g protein, 85 mg calcium, 3 mg iron

Roasted Artichokes with Vinaigrette
(recipe on facing page)

Roasted Sausage & Onion with Pita Breads

Preparation time: 15 minutes
Cooking time: About 45 minutes

- 12 ounces (340 g) mild turkey Italian sausages, cut diagonally into 1-inch (2.5-cm) lengths
- 2 large onions, cut into wedges about ½ inch (1 cm) thick
- 5 tablespoons (75 ml) balsamic vinegar
- 12 miniature pita breads (*each* about 3 inches/8 cm in diameter), cut into halves

1. In a 9- by 13-inch (23- by 33-cm) baking pan, combine sausages, onions, and ¼ cup (60 ml) of the vinegar. Bake in a 425°F (220°C) oven until sausage is well browned and almost all liquid has evaporated (about 45 minutes); stir occasionally and add water, ¼ cup (60 ml) at a time, if drippings begin to scorch.

2. Remove pan from oven and add 1 tablespoon (15 ml) water and remaining 1 tablespoon (15 ml) vinegar. Let stand for about 3 minutes; then stir to scrape browned bits free from pan bottom.

3. Transfer sausage-onion mixture to a serving dish and keep hot. To serve, spoon mixture into pita bread halves. Makes 12 servings.

Per serving: 140 calories (22% calories from fat), 3 g total fat, 0.9 g saturated fat, 15 mg cholesterol, 339 mg sodium, 20 g carbohydrates, 1 g fiber, 8 g protein, 39 mg calcium, 2 mg iron

Chili Shrimp

Preparation time: 15 minutes
Cooking time: 15 to 20 minutes

- 1 bottle or can (about 12 oz./340 g) beer
- ½ cup (85 g) finely chopped onion
- ¾ teaspoon celery seeds
- 1 dried bay leaf
- 1 pound (455 g) large raw shrimp (31 to 35 per lb.), shelled and deveined
- ½ cup (120 ml) tomato-based chili sauce
- 1 tablespoon (15 ml) honey-flavored mustard

  About 20 large fresh spinach leaves, rinsed and crisped
- 2 tablespoons drained capers

1. In a wide frying pan, combine beer, onion, celery seeds, and bay leaf. Bring to a boil over high heat; boil for 2 minutes.

Add shrimp. Reduce heat, cover, and simmer, stirring occasionally, until shrimp are just opaque in center; cut to test (about 3 minutes). With a slotted spoon, lift shrimp from pan and transfer to a large bowl.

2. Bring shrimp cooking liquid to a boil over high heat; then boil until reduced to ⅓ cup (80 ml). Remove and discard bay leaf. Add chili sauce and mustard to reduced liquid; blend well. Serve; or cover shrimp and dressing separately and refrigerate until cool (at least 1 hour) or until next day.

3. To serve, line 4 individual plates with spinach leaves; top equally with shrimp, then with dressing. Sprinkle with capers. Makes 4 servings.

Per serving: 171 calories (10% calories from fat), 2 g total fat, 0.3 g saturated fat, 140 mg cholesterol, 731 mg sodium, 17 g carbohydrates, 1 g fiber, 21 g protein, 100 mg calcium, 4 mg iron

Pickled Vegetables

Preparation time: 15 minutes
Cooking time: About 15 minutes
Chilling time: At least 1 day
Pictured on page 62

- 8 ounces (230 g) small carrots (*each* 4 to 5 inches/10 to 12.5 cm long)
- 1 package (about 10 oz./285 g) frozen tiny onions, thawed
- 1 large red bell pepper (about 8 oz./230 g), seeded and cut into strips about ½ inch (1 cm) wide
- 1 package (about 9 oz./255 g) frozen artichoke hearts, thawed
- 2 cups (470 ml) white wine vinegar
- ¾ cup (150 g) sugar
- 2 tablespoons drained capers
- 2 small dried hot red chiles
- 2 cloves garlic, peeled and crushed

1. In a 2- to 3-quart (1.9- to 2.8-liter) pan, bring 4 cups (950 ml) water to a boil over high heat. Add carrots and boil, uncovered, until barely tender when pierced (about 3 minutes); drain well.

2. In a clean, dry wide-mouth 1½- to 2-quart (1.4- to 1.9-liter) jar (or in two 1-quart jars), layer carrots, onions, bell pepper, and artichokes. Set aside.

3. In pan used to cook carrots, stir together vinegar, sugar, capers, chiles, and garlic. Bring to a boil over high heat, stirring until sugar is dissolved. Pour hot vinegar mixture

over vegetables. Cover and refrigerate for at least 1 day or up to 2 weeks. To serve, lift vegetables from marinade. Makes about 6 cups (1.4 liters).

Per ¼ cup (60 ml): 42 calories (2% calories from fat), 0.1 g total fat, 0 g saturated fat, 0 mg cholesterol, 28 mg sodium, 10 g carbohydrates, 0.9 g fiber, 0.5 g protein, 10 mg calcium, 0.2 mg iron

Wild Mushroom Polenta Boards

Preparation time: 1 hour
Cooking time: About 1 hour

- ½ cup (60 g) all-purpose flour
- ½ cup (70 g) polenta or yellow cornmeal
- ¼ cup (30 g) instant nonfat dry milk
- 1½ teaspoons baking powder
- 1 tablespoon butter or margarine
- 2 tablespoons (30 ml) olive oil or salad oil
- 1 medium-size head garlic (3 oz./85 g)
- 8 ounces (230 g) *each* fresh shiitake, chanterelle, and oyster mushrooms
- 1 tablespoon *each* chopped fresh rosemary and chopped fresh sage; or 1 teaspoon *each* dried rubbed sage and dried rosemary
- 2 teaspoons cornstarch mixed with ¾ cup (180 ml) fat-free reduced-sodium chicken broth

- 2 tablespoons grated Parmesan cheese
  Rosemary and sage sprigs

1. In a food processor or a medium-size bowl, whirl or stir together flour, polenta, dry milk, and baking powder. Add butter; whirl or rub with your fingers until mixture resembles coarse crumbs. Add ⅓ cup (80 ml) water; whirl or stir with a fork until dough begins to form a ball. Turn dough out onto a lightly floured board and pat into a ball; then knead briefly, just until dough holds together smoothly.

2. Divide dough into 6 equal portions; cover with plastic wrap. Flour board well; then, working with one piece of dough at a time, roll each piece into an irregular 6- to 7-inch (15- to 18-cm) round. As rounds are shaped, arrange them, slightly apart, on large baking sheets; cover with plastic wrap. When all rounds have been shaped, remove plastic wrap and bake polenta boards in a 350°F (175°C) oven until lightly browned (12 to 14 minutes). If made ahead, let cool completely on racks; then store airtight until next day.

3. Pour 1 tablespoon (15 ml) of the oil into a small baking pan. Cut garlic head in half crosswise

(through cloves). Place garlic, cut side down, in pan; bake in a 350°F (175°C) oven until cut side is golden brown (about 45 minutes). Using a thin spatula, lift garlic from pan and transfer to a rack; let stand until cool enough to touch (about 10 minutes). Squeeze garlic cloves from skins into a small bowl; mash garlic thoroughly.

4. While garlic is baking, trim and discard stems from shiitake mushrooms. Thinly slice shiitake mushroom caps and whole chanterelles. Place sliced shiitake and chanterelle mushrooms and whole oyster mushrooms in a 5- to 6-quart (5- to 6-liter) pan; add remaining 1 tablespoon (15 ml) oil, chopped rosemary, and chopped sage. Cover and cook over medium-high heat until mushrooms are juicy (about 8 minutes). Uncover; cook, stirring often, until almost all liquid has evaporated and mushrooms are browned (15 to 20 more minutes). Add cornstarch mixture and mashed garlic; stir until mixture boils and thickens slightly.

5. Lay polenta boards, side by side, on 2 large baking sheets. Spoon hot mushroom sauce into center of each; sprinkle evenly with cheese. Broil 4 to 6 inches (10 to 15 cm) below heat until sizzling

(about 2 minutes). With a spatula, transfer to individual plates; garnish with rosemary and sage sprigs. Makes 6 servings.

Per serving: 202 calories (30% calories from fat), 7 g total fat, 2 g saturated fat, 7 mg cholesterol, 276 mg sodium, 29 g carbohydrates, 3 g fiber, 7 g protein, 160 mg calcium, 3 mg iron

Cherry Pepper Shooters

Preparation time: 20 minutes

- 2 jars (about 1 lb./455 g *each*) mild cherry peppers, drained
- 1 can (about 8 oz./ 230 g) pineapple chunks packed in juice, drained
- 2 ounces (55 g) thinly sliced prosciutto, cut into 1½-inch (3.5-cm) squares

1. Cut off and discard pepper stems. With a small spoon, scoop out and discard seeds.

2. Cut each pineapple chunk in half; wrap each half in a piece of prosciutto. Stuff wrapped pineapple chunks into peppers. Makes 12 servings.

Per serving: 44 calories (13% calories from fat), 0.7 g total fat, 0.2 g saturated fat, 4 mg cholesterol, sodium information not available, 8 g carbohydrates, 0.1 g fiber, 1 g protein, 3 mg calcium, 1 mg iron

Italian Greens Risotto
(recipe on facing page)

Broccoli rabe (also called rapini) is a pungent, bitter green that's very popular in Italy. In this recipe, it combines with fresh asparagus in a satisfying risotto.

- 12 ounces (340 g) broccoli rabe (rapini)
- 12 ounces (340 g) asparagus, tough ends snapped off
- 4 teaspoons (20 ml) olive oil
- 1 large onion, finely chopped
- 1 cup (200 g) short- or medium-grain white rice
- 3 cups (710 ml) fat-free reduced-sodium chicken broth
- ½ cup (120 ml) dry white wine
- ½ cup (40 g) grated Parmesan cheese

1. Cut off and discard any coarse stem ends from broccoli rabe; discard any bruised or yellow leaves. If any stems are thicker than ⅜ inch (1 cm), cut them in half lengthwise. Rinse and drain broccoli rabe.

Italian Greens Risotto

Preparation time: 15 minutes
Cooking time: About 45 minutes
Pictured on facing page

2. Chop or thinly slice half each of the broccoli rabe and asparagus. Leave remaining asparagus spears and broccoli rabe leaves and flowerets whole.

3. In a wide nonstick frying pan, combine chopped broccoli rabe, chopped asparagus, and 1 tablespoon (15 ml) of the oil. Cook over medium-high heat, stirring, until vegetables are just tender to bite (about 4 minutes). Remove from pan and set aside. To pan, add ½ cup (120 ml) water, whole asparagus spears, and whole broccoli rabe leaves and flowerets. Cover and

cook, turning vegetables often with a wide spatula, until vegetables are just tender to bite (about 4 minutes). Lift from pan; set aside.

4. In same pan, combine remaining 1 teaspoon oil and onion; cook over medium-high heat, stirring often, until onion is tinged with brown (5 to 8 minutes). Add rice and stir until opaque (3 to 4 minutes). Stir in broth and wine. Bring to a boil, stirring often. Then reduce heat and simmer, uncovered, until rice is tender to bite and almost all liquid has been absorbed (about 25 minutes); stir occasionally at first, more often as mixture thickens. Stir in sautéed chopped vegetables and cheese. Spoon onto a platter; surround with whole vegetables and serve immediately. Makes 6 servings.

Per serving: 237 calories (22% calories from fat), 5 g total fat, 2 g saturated fat, 5 mg cholesterol, 480 mg sodium, 35 g carbohydrates, 3 g fiber, 10 g protein, 154 mg calcium, 3 mg iron

---

Bold with onions and Gorgonzola cheese, this mushroom risotto is good with juicy steaks or chops.

- 1 teaspoon olive oil
- 8 ounces (230 g) mushrooms, thinly sliced
- 1 large onion, chopped
- 1 clove garlic, minced
- 1 cup (200 g) short- or medium-grain white rice
- ¼ teaspoon *each* dried thyme, dried marjoram, and dried rubbed sage
- 3 cups (790 ml) fat-free reduced-sodium chicken broth
- ½ cup (125 g) packed crumbled Gorgonzola or other blue-veined cheese

Risotto with Mushrooms

Preparation time: 15 minutes
Cooking time: About 45 minutes

- 1 teaspoon dry sherry (or to taste)

1. Heat oil in a wide nonstick frying pan over medium heat. Add mushrooms, onion, and garlic. Cook, stirring often, until vegetables are soft and are beginning to stick to pan bottom (about 15 minutes); add water, 1 tablespoon (15 ml) at a

time, if pan drippings begin to scorch.

2. Add rice, thyme, marjoram, and sage; stir until rice is opaque (3 to 4 minutes). Stir in broth. Bring to a boil, stirring often. Then reduce heat and simmer, uncovered, until rice is tender to bite and almost all liquid has been absorbed (about 25 minutes); stir occasionally at first, more often as mixture thickens.

3. Remove rice mixture from heat and stir in cheese and sherry. Makes 4 to 6 servings.

Per serving: 230 calories (19% calories from fat), 5 g total fat, 3 g saturated fat, 10 mg cholesterol, 450 mg sodium, 38 g carbohydrates, 2 g fiber, 8 g protein, 76 mg calcium, 2 mg iron

Here's risotto in a new guise: it's formed into patties, pan-fried until crisp, and served with a tomato-basil purée.

- 2 tablespoons (30 ml) olive oil; or 2 tablespoons butter
- 1¼ cups (244 g) short- or medium-grain white rice
- 1¾ cups (420 ml) fat-free reduced-sodium chicken broth
- 5 to 6 ounces (140 to 170 g) mozzarella cheese, shredded
- ¼ cup (20 g) grated Parmesan cheese
- 4 green onions, finely chopped
- 1 can (about 14½ oz./415 g) diced tomatoes
- ¼ cup (60 ml) plain nonfat yogurt
- ¼ cup (10 g) coarsely chopped fresh basil
  Basil sprigs

1. Heat 1 tablespoon (15 ml) of the oil in a 3- to 4-quart (2.8- to 3.8-liter) pan over medium-high heat.

Risotto Cakes with Tomato Purée

Preparation time: 25 minutes
Cooking time: About 1¼ hours

Add rice and stir until opaque (3 to 4 minutes). Stir in broth and 1½ cups (360 ml) water. Bring to a boil, stirring often. Then reduce heat and simmer, uncovered, until rice is tender to bite and almost all liquid has been absorbed (25 to 30 minutes); stir occasionally at first, more often as mixture thickens. Remove from heat and stir in mozzarella cheese, Parmesan cheese, and onions. Let cool uncovered. (At this point, you may cover and refrigerate until next day.)

2. In a food processor or blender, combine tomatoes and their liquid, yogurt, and chopped basil. Whirl until smoothly puréed; set aside.

3. Divide rice mixture into 12 equal portions; shape each portion into a cake about ¾ inch (2 cm) thick. Heat 1 teaspoon of the oil in a wide nonstick frying pan over medium-high heat. Add risotto cakes to pan, a portion at a time (do not crowd pan); cook, turning once, until golden on both sides (about 20 minutes). Add remaining 2 teaspoons oil to pan as needed. As cakes are cooked, arrange them in a single layer in a large, shallow baking pan; cover loosely with foil and keep warm in a 300°F (150°C) oven until all cakes have been cooked.

4. To serve, arrange cakes on individual plates; top with tomato purée and garnish with basil sprigs. Makes 6 servings.

Per serving: 286 calories (28% calories from fat), 9 g total fat, 3 g saturated fat, 12 mg cholesterol, 507 mg sodium, 38 g carbohydrates, 1 g fiber, 13 g protein, 313 mg calcium, 3 mg iron

---

Tangy dried tomatoes and sliced mushrooms dot this lively pilaf.

- 1 tablespoon (15 ml) olive oil
- 8 ounces (230 g) portabella or button mushrooms, sliced
- 1 medium-size onion, chopped
- 1 cup (185 g) long-grain white rice
- 2½ cups (590 ml) fat-free reduced-sodium chicken broth
- ¾ cup (about 1½ oz./43 g) dried tomatoes (not packed in oil), chopped
- ¼ cup (10 g) chopped cilantro
  Salt and pepper

Dried Tomato Pilaf

Preparation time: 15 minutes
Cooking time: 35 to 45 minutes

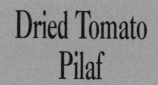

1. Heat oil in a 3- to 4-quart (2.8- to 3.8-liter) pan over medium-high heat. Add mushrooms and onion; cook, stirring often, until almost all liquid has evaporated and vegetables are lightly browned (10 to 12 minutes).

2. Add rice and stir until opaque (3 to 4 minutes). Add broth and tomatoes. Bring to a boil; then reduce heat, cover, and simmer until rice is tender to bite (20 to 25 minutes). Stir in cilantro. Season to taste with salt and pepper. Makes 6 servings.

Per serving: 181 calories (13% calories from fat), 3 g total fat, 0.4 g saturated fat, 0 mg cholesterol, 280 mg sodium, 34 g carbohydrates, 3 g fiber, 6 g protein, 17 mg calcium, 2 mg iron

If you can't find small peppers, just cut medium-size ones down: slice the tops off the peppers as directed, then trim the cut edges of both top and bottom pieces so the whole peppers will be just 2 to 3 inches tall when reassembled.

- 10 to 12 very small red, yellow, or orange bell peppers (*each 2 to 3 inches/5 to 8 cm tall*)
- 1 cup (200 g) short- or medium-grain white rice
- 4 teaspoons grated lemon peel
- 8 ounces (230 g) sliced bacon, crisply cooked, drained, and crumbled
- ¼ cup (43 g) drained capers
- ¼ cup (60 ml) seasoned rice vinegar

Red Bell Peppers Stuffed with Caper Rice

Preparation time: 20 minutes
Cooking time: 35 to 40 minutes

1. Cut off the top third of each pepper. With a small spoon, scoop out seeds and white membranes from pepper bases and tops; rinse and drain both bases and tops. If needed, trim pepper bases (without piercing them) so they will sit steadily.

2. In a 2- to 3-quart (1.9- to 2.8-liter) pan, combine rice, lemon peel, and

2½ cups (590 ml) water. Bring to a boil over high heat. Reduce heat, cover, and simmer until rice is tender to bite and almost all liquid has been absorbed (about 20 minutes). Remove from heat. With a fork, stir in bacon, capers, and vinegar.

3. Set pepper bases upright, spacing them slightly apart, in a shallow 10- by 15-inch (25- by 38-cm) baking pan. Mound rice mixture equally in pepper bases; set pepper tops in place. Bake in a 450°F (230°C) oven until peppers are blistered and rice mixture is hot in center (8 to 12 minutes). Makes 10 to 12 servings.

Per serving: 131 calories (21% calories from fat), 3 g total fat, 1 g saturated fat, 5 mg cholesterol, 263 mg sodium, 22 g carbohydrates, 2 g fiber, 4 g protein, 12 mg calcium, 1 mg iron

---

Creamy polenta is enhanced by an easy sauce based on fresh tomatoes, yellow bell peppers, and basil.

- 3 pounds (1.35 kg) pear-shaped (Roma-type) tomatoes, peeled (if desired) and coarsely chopped
- 2 large yellow bell peppers (about 1 lb./455 g *total*), seeded and chopped
- 1 cup (40 g) lightly packed slivered fresh basil or ¼ cup (8 g) dried basil
- 2 cloves garlic, minced
- 2 cups (470 ml) low-fat (2%) milk
- ½ cup (120 ml) canned vegetable broth
- 1 cup (138 g) polenta or yellow cornmeal
- 1 teaspoon chopped fresh sage or ¼ teaspoon ground sage

Polenta with Fresh Tomato Sauce

Preparation time: 25 minutes
Cooking time: About 20 minutes

- ½ teaspoon salt
- ½ cup (40 g) grated Parmesan cheese
- Basil sprigs

1. In a 3- to 4-quart (2.8- to 3.8-liter) pan, combine two-thirds each of the tomatoes and bell peppers, half the slivered basil, and all the garlic. Cook over medium-high heat, stirring often, until tomatoes begin to fall apart (15 to 20 minutes).

2. Meanwhile, in a 4- to 5-quart (3.8- to 5-liter) pan, bring milk and broth just to a boil over medium-high heat. Stir in polenta, sage, and salt. Reduce heat and simmer, uncovered, stirring often and scraping bottom of pan with a long-handled spoon (mixture will spatter), until polenta tastes creamy (about 15 minutes). Remove pan from heat; stir in cheese. Keep warm.

3. Working quickly, stir remaining tomatoes, bell peppers, and slivered basil into sauce. Divide polenta equally among deep individual bowls and top with sauce. Garnish with basil sprigs. Makes 4 servings.

Per serving: 346 calories (19% calories from fat), 7 g total fat, 4 g saturated fat, 18 mg cholesterol, 681 mg sodium, 58 g carbohydrates, 8 g fiber, 16 g protein, 414 mg calcium, 5 mg iron

Toasted hazelnuts and crisp, hazelnut-seasoned crumbs flavor these simple poached leeks.

Poached Leeks with Hazelnuts

Preparation time: 25 minutes
Cooking time: 20 to 25 minutes

¼ cup (34 g) hazelnuts

3 slices sourdough sandwich bread (about 3 oz./85 g *total*), torn into pieces

2 cloves garlic, minced or pressed

¼ teaspoon dried thyme

1 teaspoon hazelnut oil or olive oil

8 medium-size leeks (about 4 lbs./ 1.8 kg *total*)
   Balsamic vinegar

1. Spread hazelnuts in a single layer in a shallow baking pan. Bake in a 375°F (190°C) oven until nuts are golden beneath skins (about 10 minutes). Let nuts cool slightly; then pour into a towel, fold to enclose, and rub to remove as much of loose skins as possible. Let cool; then coarsely chop and set aside.

2. While nuts are toasting, in a food processor or blender, whirl bread to form fine crumbs. Pour crumbs into a medium-size nonstick frying pan and add garlic and thyme. Drizzle with oil and 1 tablespoon (15 ml) water. Then stir over medium-high heat until crumbs are lightly browned (5 to 7 minutes). Remove from pan and set aside.

3. Trim and discard roots and tough tops from leeks; remove and discard coarse outer leaves. Split leeks lengthwise. Thoroughly rinse leek halves between layers; tie each half with string to hold it together.

4. In a 5- to 6-quart (5- to 6-liter) pan, bring 8 cups (1.9 liters) water to a boil over high heat. Add leeks; reduce heat, cover, and simmer until tender when pierced (5 to 7 minutes). Carefully transfer leeks to a strainer; let drain. Snip and discard strings; arrange leeks on a platter. Sprinkle with crumb mixture, then hazelnuts; offer vinegar to add to taste. Makes 4 to 6 servings.

Per serving: 185 calories (25% calories from fat), 5 g total fat, 0.5 g saturated fat, 0 mg cholesterol, 134 mg sodium, 31 g carbohydrates, 3 g fiber, 5 g protein, 115 mg calcium, 4 mg iron

---

For a colorful side dish, present this quintet of richly browned roasted vegetables.

Roasted Vegetable Medley

Preparation time: 30 minutes
Cooking time: About 45 minutes
Pictured on facing page

1 large beet (about 8 oz./230 g), peeled

2 small red thin-skinned potatoes (about 8 oz./230 g *total*)

1 medium-size sweet potato or yam (about 8 oz./230 g), peeled

2 large carrots (about 8 oz./ 230 g *total*)

1 small red onion (about 8 oz./ 230 g)

5 teaspoons (25 ml) olive oil

2 tablespoons *each* chopped fresh oregano and chopped fresh basil; or 2 teaspoons *each* dried oregano and dried basil

1 or 2 cloves garlic, minced or pressed

¼ cup (20 g) grated Parmesan cheese
   Oregano and basil sprigs
   Salt

1. Cut beet, unpeeled thin-skinned potatoes, and sweet potato into ¾-inch (2-cm) chunks. Cut carrots diagonally into ½-inch (1-cm) pieces; cut onion into ¾-inch (2-cm) wedges. Combine all vegetables in a shallow 10- by 15-inch (25- by 38-cm) baking pan; drizzle with oil and toss to coat vegetables evenly with oil.

2. Bake in a 475°F (245°C) oven until vegetables are richly browned and tender when pierced (35 to 45 minutes), stirring occasionally. Watch carefully to prevent scorching. As pieces brown, remove them and keep warm; add water, ¼ cup (60 ml) at a time, if pan appears dry.

3. Transfer vegetables to a platter or serving dish and sprinkle with chopped oregano, chopped basil, garlic, and a little of the cheese. Garnish with oregano and basil sprigs. Season to taste with salt and remaining cheese. Makes 6 servings.

Per serving: 162 calories (28% calories from fat), 5 g total fat, 1 g saturated fat, 3 mg cholesterol, 104 mg sodium, 26 g carbohydrates, 4 g fiber, 4 g protein, 87 mg calcium, 1 mg iron

Roasted Vegetable Medley
(recipe on facing page)

Shell & Bean Soup

Preparation time: 20 minutes
Cooking time: About 20 minutes

....

1 small red onion (about 8 oz./230 g), chopped

1 teaspoon olive oil

1 cup (120 g) chopped celery

4 cloves garlic, chopped

10 cups (2.4 liters) fat-free reduced-sodium chicken broth

1½ cups (173 g) dried small pasta shells

3 to 4 cups (555 to 740 g) cooked or canned white beans, drained and rinsed

1 cup (110 g) shredded carrots

1 package (about 10 oz./285 g) frozen tiny peas

½ cup (40 g) grated Parmesan cheese

....

1. Set aside ⅓ cup (57 g) of the chopped onion. In a 6- to 8-quart (6- to 8-liter) pan, combine remaining onion, oil, celery, and garlic. Cook over medium-high heat, stirring often, until onion is lightly browned (5 to 8 minutes). Add broth and bring to a boil. Stir in pasta and beans; reduce heat, cover, and simmer until pasta is almost tender to bite (5 to 7 minutes). Add carrots and peas; bring to a boil.

2. Ladle soup into individual bowls; sprinkle equally with cheese and reserved onion. Makes 6 to 8 servings.

Per serving: 324 calories (9% calories from fat), 3 g total fat, 1 g saturated fat, 5 mg cholesterol, 1,113 mg sodium, 53 g carbohydrates, 7 g fiber, 22 g protein, 194 mg calcium, 5 mg iron

Roasted Vegetable & Cheese Soup

Preparation time: 25 minutes
Cooking time: About 30 minutes

....

2 medium-size leeks (about 1 lb./455 g)

1 large ear corn (about 10 inches/25 cm long), husk and silk removed

1 small red onion (about 8 oz./230 g), cut in half

1 large red bell pepper (about 8 oz./ 230 g)

1 large yellow or green bell pepper (about 8 oz./230 g)

2 cloves garlic, peeled

4 cups (950 ml) fat-free reduced-sodium chicken broth

1 cup (about 4 oz./115 g) shredded reduced-fat sharp Cheddar cheese

¼ cup (60 ml) nonfat sour cream

....

1. Trim and discard roots and tough tops from leeks; remove and discard coarse outer leaves. Split leeks lengthwise; thoroughly rinse leek halves between layers. In a large, shallow baking pan, arrange leeks, corn, onion halves, and whole bell peppers.

2. Broil 4 to 6 inches (10 to 15 cm) below heat, turning vegetables as needed to brown evenly, for 10 minutes. Add garlic. Continue to broil, turning as needed, until vegetables are well charred (about 5 more minutes); remove vegetables from pan as they are charred. Cover vegetables loosely with foil and let stand until cool enough to handle (about 10 minutes).

3. With a sharp knife, cut corn kernels from cob. Remove and discard skins, seeds, and stems from bell peppers. Coarsely chop peppers, leeks, onion, and garlic.

4. In a 4- to 5-quart (3.8- to 5-liter) pan, combine vegetables and broth. Bring to a boil over high heat; then reduce heat, cover, and simmer for 10 minutes to blend flavors. Ladle soup into individual bowls; sprinkle with cheese, top with sour cream, and serve. Makes 4 servings.

Per serving: 231 calories (22% calories from fat), 6 g total fat, 4 g saturated fat, 30 mg cholesterol, 901 mg sodium, 30 g carbohydrates, 5 g fiber, 18 g protein, 331 mg calcium, 2 mg iron

Minestrone with Parsley Pesto

Preparation time: 25 minutes
Cooking time: About 30 minutes

- 3 quarts (2.8 liters) fat-free reduced-sodium chicken broth
- 2 ounces (55 g) thinly sliced prosciutto or bacon, chopped
- 2 tablespoons salted roasted almonds
- 2 cups (120 g) lightly packed Italian or regular parsley sprigs
- 2 tablespoons (30 ml) *each* olive oil and white wine vinegar
- 2 teaspoons honey
- 1 clove garlic, peeled
- 1 tablespoon drained capers
- ⅛ to ¼ teaspoon crushed red pepper flakes
- 1½ cups (225 g) diced unpeeled red thin-skinned potatoes
- 1 cup (120 g) sliced celery
- 1 large zucchini (about 8 oz./230 g), cut into ½-inch (1-cm) slices
- 10 ounces (285 g) fresh Italian green beans, cut into 1-inch (2.5-cm) lengths; or 1 package (about 10 oz./285 g) frozen Italian green beans, thawed
- 1 large red or yellow bell pepper (about 8 oz./230 g), seeded and cut into ½-inch (1-cm) chunks
- ¾ cup (85 g) dried salad or elbow macaroni
- 1 cup (53 g) lightly packed shredded radicchio or red Swiss chard
- ½ cup (50 g) thinly sliced green onions

1. In a 5- to 6-quart (5- to 6-liter) pan, combine broth and prosciutto. Bring to a rolling boil over high heat (10 to 12 minutes).

2. Meanwhile, in a food processor or blender, combine almonds, parsley sprigs, oil, vinegar, honey, garlic, capers, red pepper flakes, and 1 tablespoon (15 ml) water. Whirl until coarsely puréed; scrape sides of container as needed and add 1 to 2 tablespoons (15 to 30 ml) more water if pesto is too thick. Transfer pesto to a small bowl and set aside.

3. Add potatoes to boiling broth; reduce heat, cover, and simmer for 10 minutes. Add celery, zucchini, beans, bell pepper, and pasta; cover and simmer until potatoes and pasta are tender to bite (about 5 more minutes).

4. Stir in radicchio and onions; simmer until radicchio is limp but still bright red (about 4 minutes). Serve immediately; offer parsley pesto to spoon into individual servings. Makes 8 servings.

Per serving: 180 calories (29% calories from fat), 6 g total fat, 0.9 g saturated fat, 6 mg cholesterol, 1,172 mg sodium, 22 g carbohydrates, 3 g fiber, 11 g protein, 66 mg calcium, 3 mg iron

Tomato Fava Soup

Preparation time: 25 minutes
Cooking time: About 30 minutes

- 2 tablespoons (30 ml) olive oil
- 1 large onion, chopped
- 1½ pounds (680 g) ripe tomatoes, quartered
- 2 tablespoons finely chopped fresh savory or 1 teaspoon dried savory
- ¾ teaspoon sugar
- ¼ teaspoon pepper
- 2 cups shelled fava beans (about 2 lbs./905 g in the pod); see Note at right
- 4 cups (950 ml) fat-free reduced-sodium chicken broth

1. Heat oil in a 3- to 4-quart (2.8- to 3.8-liter) pan over medium-high heat. Add onion and cook, stirring often, until it begins to brown (5 to 10 minutes). Add tomatoes, savory, sugar, and pepper. Bring to a boil; then reduce heat and simmer, uncovered, until tomatoes are very soft when pressed (about 15 minutes).

2. Meanwhile, in a 2- to 3-quart (1.9- to 2.8-liter) pan, bring 4 cups (950 ml) water to a boil over high heat. Add beans and simmer, uncovered, until just tender when pierced (3 to 5 minutes). Drain, then let stand until cool enough to touch. With your fingers, slip skins from beans; discard skins and set beans aside.

3. In a food processor or blender, whirl tomato mixture until coarsely puréed. Return to pan and add broth; stir over high heat until hot. Ladle soup into individual bowls; sprinkle beans equally over each serving. Makes 6 servings.

Note: A few people, typically of Mediterranean descent, have a severe allergic reaction to fava beans and their pollen. If favas are new to you, check your family history before eating them.

Per serving: 261 calories (19% calories from fat), 6 g total fat, 0.8 g saturated fat, 0 mg cholesterol, 447 mg sodium, 39 g carbohydrates, 9 g fiber, 17 g protein, 70 mg calcium, 4 mg iron

Pesto Pasta Salad
(recipe on facing page)

Fragrant pesto dressing flavors a good-looking pasta salad dotted with dried tomatoes.

- 1 cup (about 2 oz./55 g) dried tomatoes (not packed in oil)
- 2 tablespoons pine nuts
- 1 pound (455 g) dried medium-size pasta shells or elbow macaroni
- 1 cup (45 g) firmly packed chopped fresh spinach
- 3 tablespoons dried basil
- 1 or 2 cloves garlic, peeled
- ⅓ cup (30 g) grated Parmesan cheese
- ¼ cup (60 ml) olive oil
- 1 teaspoon Oriental sesame oil
  Salt and pepper

1. Place tomatoes in a small bowl

Pesto Pasta Salad

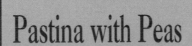

Preparation time: 20 minutes
Cooking time: About 15 minutes
Pictured on facing page

and add boiling water to cover. Let stand until soft (about 10 minutes), stirring occasionally. Drain well; gently squeeze out excess liquid. Cut tomatoes into thin slivers and set aside.

2. While tomatoes are soaking, toast pine nuts in a small frying pan over medium heat until golden (about 3 minutes), stirring often. Pour out of pan and set aside.

3. In a 6- to 8-quart (6- to 8-liter) pan, bring 4 quarts (3.8 liters) water to a boil over medium-high heat;

stir in pasta and cook until just tender to bite, 8 to 10 minutes. (Or cook pasta according to package directions.) Drain, rinse with cold water until cool, and drain well again. Pour into a large serving bowl.

4. In a food processor or blender, whirl spinach, basil, garlic, cheese, olive oil, sesame oil, and 1 teaspoon water until smoothly puréed; scrape sides of container as needed and add a little more water if pesto is too thick.

5. Add tomatoes and spinach pesto to pasta; mix well. Sprinkle with pine nuts; season to taste with salt and pepper. Makes 8 servings.

Per serving: 332 calories (28% calories from fat), 10 g total fat, 2 g saturated fat, 3 mg cholesterol, 78 mg sodium, 49 g carbohydrates, 3 g fiber, 11 g protein, 98 mg calcium, 3 mg iron

---

For a refreshing side dish, serve this combination of tiny pasta beads, sweet peas, and mint-lemon dressing.

- 2 ounces (55 g) thinly sliced prosciutto or bacon, cut into thin strips
- 1½ cups (340 g) dried orzo or other tiny rice-shaped pasta
- 1 package (about 1 lb./455 g) frozen tiny peas
- ¼ cup (25 g) thinly sliced green onions
- ¼ cup (10 g) chopped fresh mint
- ¼ cup (60 ml) olive oil
- 1 teaspoon finely shredded lemon peel
- 2 tablespoons (30 ml) lemon juice
  Mint sprigs
  Pepper

Pastina with Peas

Preparation time: 15 minutes
Cooking time: About 20 minutes

1. In a wide nonstick frying pan, cook prosciutto over medium-high heat, stirring often, just until crisp (about 3 minutes). Remove from pan and set aside.

2. In a 5- to 6-quart (5- to 6-liter) pan, bring about 3 quarts (2.8 liters) water to a boil over medium-high heat; stir in pasta and cook until just tender to bite, about 8 minutes. (Or cook pasta according to package directions.) Drain, rinse with cold water until cool, and drain well again. Pour pasta into a large serving bowl; add peas, onions, and chopped mint. Mix gently.

3. In a small bowl, beat oil, lemon peel, and lemon juice until blended. Add to pasta mixture; mix gently but thoroughly. Sprinkle with prosciutto and garnish with mint sprigs. Season to taste with pepper. Makes 6 servings.

Per serving: 364 calories (28% calories from fat), 12 g total fat, 2 g saturated fat, 8 mg cholesterol, 282 mg sodium, 52 g carbohydrates, 4 g fiber, 14 g protein, 29 mg calcium, 3 mg iron

Pasta & Cheese Pie

Smoked mozzarella or Gouda cheese gives this vegetable-pasta pie an especially savory flavor.

Preparation time: 25 minutes
Cooking time: About 35 minutes

8 ounces (230 g) mushrooms, thinly sliced

1 large red bell pepper (about 8 oz./230 g), seeded and coarsely chopped

1 large onion, chopped

4 cloves garlic, minced

½ cup (120 ml) low-fat (2%) milk

2 teaspoons cornstarch

2 large eggs

6 large egg whites

¾ cup (85 g) shredded smoked part-skim mozzarella or smoked Gouda cheese

¼ cup (20 g) grated Parmesan cheese

2 tablespoons chopped fresh thyme or 1½ teaspoons dried thyme

¼ teaspoon salt

⅛ teaspoon crushed red pepper flakes

3 cups (405 g) cold cooked spaghetti

1 teaspoon olive oil
Thyme sprigs

1. In a wide nonstick frying pan, combine mushrooms, bell pepper, onion, garlic, and ⅓ cup (80 ml) water. Cook over medium-high heat, stirring occasionally, until mushrooms are soft and almost all liquid has evaporated (about 10 minutes). Remove from pan.

2. In a large bowl, blend milk and cornstarch. Add eggs and egg whites and beat well. Stir in mozzarella cheese, Parmesan cheese, chopped thyme, salt, and red pepper flakes. Add pasta and mushroom mixture to egg mixture; lift with 2 forks to mix well. Set aside.

3. Place a 9-inch-round (23-cm-round) baking pan (do not use a nonstick pan) in oven while it heats to 500°F (260°C). When pan is hot (after about 5 minutes), carefully remove it from oven and pour in oil, tilting pan to coat. Mix pasta mixture again; then transfer to pan and press lightly to make an even layer.

4. Bake on lowest rack of oven until top of pie is tinged with brown and center feels firm when lightly pressed (about 20 minutes). To serve, cut pie into 6 wedges; transfer each wedge to an individual plate and garnish with thyme sprigs. Makes 6 servings.

Per serving: 248 calories (25% calories from fat), 7 g total fat, 3 g saturated fat, 85 mg cholesterol, 309 mg sodium, 31 g carbohydrates, 3 g fiber, 16 g protein, 201 mg calcium, 2 mg iron

Asparagus with Garlic Crumbs

Crisp, garlicky bread crumbs enhance cooked, cooled spring asparagus in this easy dish.

Preparation time: 15 minutes
Cooking time: About 25 minutes

3 slices sourdough sandwich bread (about 3 oz./85 g *total*), torn into pieces

2 teaspoons olive oil

2 cloves garlic, minced or pressed

36 thick asparagus spears (about 3 lbs./1.35 kg *total*), tough ends snapped off
Salt and pepper

1. In a blender or food processor, whirl bread to form fine crumbs. Pour crumbs into a wide nonstick frying pan; add oil and garlic. Cook over medium-high heat, stirring often, until crumbs are lightly browned (5 to 7 minutes). Remove from pan and set aside.

2. Trim ends of asparagus spears so that spears are all the same length (reserve scraps for soups or salads). For the sweetest flavor and most tender texture, peel spears with a vegetable peeler.

3. In frying pan, bring about 1 inch (2.5 cm) water to a boil over medium-high heat. Add a third of the asparagus and cook, uncovered, until just tender when pierced (about 4 minutes). Lift from pan with a slotted spoon and place in a bowl of ice water to cool. Repeat with remaining asparagus, cooking it in 2 batches.

4. Drain cooled asparagus well; then arrange on a large platter. Sprinkle with crumb mixture; season to taste with salt and pepper. Makes 8 servings.

Per serving: 70 calories (20% calories from fat), 2 g total fat, 0.3 g saturated fat, 0 mg cholesterol, 68 mg sodium, 11 g carbohydrates, 2 g fiber, 5 g protein, 39 mg calcium, 1 mg iron

Fruited Spinach Purée

Preparation time: 15 minutes
Cooking time: About 10 minutes

This silky, basil-seasoned purée of sautéed spinach and pears is particularly good with roast leg of lamb.

1 package (about 10 oz./285 g) prewashed spinach leaves

1 teaspoon olive oil

4 large Anjou pears (about 2 lbs./905 g *total*), peeled, cored, and thinly sliced

¼ cup (60 ml) half-and-half

1 tablespoon dried basil

½ teaspoon *each* grated lemon peel and Oriental sesame oil

About ¼ teaspoon salt (or to taste)

1 to 2 teaspoons finely shredded lemon peel

1. Discard coarse stems and any yellow or bruised leaves from spinach. Rinse remaining spinach leaves, drain, and set aside.

2. Heat ½ teaspoon of the olive oil in a wide nonstick frying pan over medium-high heat. Add pears and cook, stirring occasionally, until almost tender when pierced (3 to 5 minutes). Transfer pears and any pan juices to a food processor or blender; keep warm.

3. Heat remaining ½ teaspoon olive oil in pan. Add spinach, a handful at a time, and cook, stirring, just until wilted; add water, 1 table-spoon (15 ml) at a time, if pan appears dry. As spinach is cooked, transfer it to a bowl; keep warm. When all spinach has been cooked, press it with the back of a wooden spoon to remove excess liquid; discard as much liquid as possible.

4. At once, transfer spinach to food processor with pears and whirl until mixture is coarsely puréed. Add half-and-half, basil, grated lemon peel, sesame oil, and salt. Whirl just until smooth but still firm enough to mound on a plate (do not overprocess). Spoon purée onto individual plates, garnish with shredded lemon peel, and serve immediately. Makes 4 to 6 servings.

Per serving: 138 calories (21% calories from fat), 4 g total fat, 1 g saturated fat, 4 mg cholesterol, 146 mg sodium, 28 g carbohydrates, 5 g fiber, 2 g protein, 92 mg calcium, 2 mg iron

Roasted Eggplant with Bell Peppers

Preparation time: 25 minutes
Cooking time: 30 to 40 minutes

Served at room temperature, this easy-to-assemble side dish is appealingly simple: just roasted eggplant, bell peppers, and garlic, dressed with a splash of balsamic vinegar.

2 large red bell peppers (about 1 lb./455 g *total*)

3 large heads garlic (about 12 oz./340 g *total*)

1 medium-size eggplant (about 1 lb./ 455 g), unpeeled, cut into 2-inch (5-cm) pieces

2 teaspoons olive oil

3 tablespoons (45 ml) balsamic vinegar

2 tablespoons chopped Italian or regular parsley

Salt and pepper

1. Cut bell peppers lengthwise into halves and arrange, cut side down, in a shallow baking pan. Broil 4 to 6 inches (10 to 15 cm) below heat until skins are charred (about 8 minutes). Cover loosely with foil and let stand until cool enough to handle (about 10 minutes).

2. Meanwhile, separate garlic heads into cloves; peel garlic cloves. Place garlic in a shallow 10- by 15-inch (25- by 38-cm) baking pan; add eggplant and oil. Mix to coat vegetables with oil. Bake in a 475°F (245°C) oven until eggplant is richly browned and soft when pressed, and garlic is tinged with brown (20 to 30 minutes). Watch carefully to prevent scorching; remove pieces as they brown and add water, ¼ cup (60 ml) at a time, if pan appears dry.

3. While eggplant is cooking, remove and discard skins, seeds, and stems from bell peppers. Cut peppers into chunks, place in a large serving bowl, and set aside.

4. Add eggplant, garlic, and vinegar to bowl with peppers; mix gently but thoroughly. Sprinkle with parsley; season to taste with salt and pepper. Serve at room temperature. Makes 4 to 6 servings.

Per serving: 149 calories (13% calories from fat), 2 g total fat, 0.3 g saturated fat, 0 mg cholesterol, 16 mg sodium, 30 g carbohydrates, 4 g fiber, 5 g protein, 148 mg calcium, 2 mg iron

Try this rosy, piquant dish with smoky grilled fish or chicken.

....

1 small red onion (about 8 oz./230 g), thinly sliced

¼ cup (60 ml) red wine vinegar

1 small European cucumber (about 12 oz./340 g)

1¼ pounds (565 g) firm-ripe pear-shaped (Roma-type) tomatoes, peeled, cut into chunks, and drained well

1 can (about 15 oz./425 g) cannellini (white kidney beans), drained and rinsed

½ cup (120 ml) balsamic vinegar

3 tablespoons firmly packed brown sugar

1½ tablespoons drained capers

½ teaspoon *each* coriander seeds and mustard seeds

¼ teaspoon fennel seeds

Tomato Compote with Seeded Vinaigrette

....

Preparation time: 20 minutes, plus
20 to 30 minutes to crisp onion
Cooking time: About 5 minutes
Marinating time: 20 minutes

....

2 tablespoons chopped Italian or regular parsley

....

1. Place onion in a medium-size bowl and add enough water to cover. Squeeze onion with your hands to bruise slightly; drain. Add 4 cups (455 g) ice cubes, 2 cups (470 ml) water, and wine vinegar. Let stand until onion is crisp (20 to 30 minutes). Drain well; discard any unmelted ice cubes.

2. While onion is soaking, cut cucumber in half lengthwise; then set halves cut side down and thinly slice crosswise. Place cucumber in a large bowl; add tomatoes and beans. Set aside.

3. In a medium-size pan, combine balsamic vinegar, sugar, capers, coriander seeds, mustard seeds, and fennel seeds. Bring to a boil over high heat; immediately pour over vegetables in bowl. Let stand for 20 minutes, stirring gently once or twice. Just before serving, stir in onion and parsley. Makes 6 to 8 servings.

....

Per serving: 105 calories (6% calories from fat), 0.8 g total fat, 0.1 g saturated fat, 0 mg cholesterol, 137 mg sodium, 21 g carbohydrates, 4 g fiber, 5 g protein, 43 mg calcium, 1 mg iron

---

Garbanzos in a ripe-olive pesto taste great atop juicy sliced tomatoes.

....

4 slices sourdough sandwich bread (about 4 oz./115 g *total*), cut into ½-inch (1-cm) cubes

5 large tomatoes (about 2½ lbs./ 1.15 kg *total*), thinly sliced

1 cup (113 g) pitted ripe olives, drained

3 tablespoons drained capers

4 teaspoons (20 ml) lemon juice

2 teaspoons *each* Oriental sesame oil and Dijon mustard

1 tablespoon (15 ml) honey (or to taste)

2 or 3 cloves garlic, peeled

¼ cup (10 g) finely chopped fresh basil

Garbanzo Beans with Olive Pesto

....

Preparation time: 15 minutes
Cooking time: 15 to 20 minutes
Pictured on facing page

....

3 tablespoons grated Parmesan cheese

2 cans (about 15 oz./425 g *each*) garbanzo beans, drained and rinsed

Basil sprigs

....

1. Spread bread cubes in a single layer in a shallow baking pan. Bake in a 325°F (165°C) oven, stirring occasionally, until crisp and lightly browned (15 to 20 minutes). Set aside.

2. Arrange tomato slices, overlapping if necessary, in a large, shallow serving bowl. Set aside.

3. In a food processor or blender, combine olives, capers, lemon juice, oil, mustard, honey, and garlic; whirl until coarsely puréed, scraping sides of container as needed. With a spoon, stir in chopped basil and cheese. Transfer olive pesto to a large bowl; add beans and two-thirds of the croutons. Mix gently but thoroughly.

4. Spoon bean salad over tomatoes; sprinkle with remaining croutons. Garnish with basil sprigs. Makes 4 to 6 servings.

....

Per serving: 286 calories (29% calories from fat), 10 g total fat, 2 g saturated fat, 2 mg cholesterol, 803 mg sodium, 41 g carbohydrates, 9 g fiber, 11 g protein, 147 g calcium, 5 mg iron

Garbanzo Beans with Olive Pesto
(recipe on facing page)

Mixed Greens with Pesto Dressing

Preparation time: 20 minutes
Cooking time: About 15 minutes

- 1 tablespoon pine nuts
- 2 teaspoons Oriental sesame oil
- 1 clove garlic, minced or pressed
- 3 slices Italian or sourdough sandwich bread (about 3 oz./85 g *total*), cut into ½-inch (1-cm) cubes
- ¼ cup (10 g) chopped fresh basil
- ¼ cup (15 g) chopped Italian or regular parsley
- 1 cup (240 ml) nonfat sour cream
- 1 tablespoon (15 ml) white wine vinegar
- 1 teaspoon honey
- 1 or 2 cloves garlic, peeled
  Salt and pepper
- 8 ounces/230 g (about 8 cups) mixed salad greens, rinsed and crisped

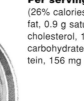

1. Toast pine nuts in a wide nonstick frying pan over medium heat until golden (about 3 minutes), stirring often. Pour out of pan and set aside. In same pan (with pan off heat), combine 1 teaspoon of the oil, garlic, and 1 tablespoon (15 ml) water. Add bread cubes and toss gently to coat. Place pan over medium heat; cook, stirring occasionally, until croutons are crisp and tinged with brown (about 10 minutes). Remove from pan and set aside.

2. In a food processor or blender, combine basil, parsley, sour cream, vinegar, honey, remaining 1 teaspoon oil, and garlic; whirl until smoothly puréed. Season to taste with salt and pepper; set aside.

3. Place greens in a large bowl; add dressing and mix gently but thoroughly. Add croutons and mix again. Sprinkle with pine nuts. Makes 4 servings.

Per serving: 154 calories (26% calories from fat), 4 g total fat, 0.9 g saturated fat, 0 mg cholesterol, 177 mg sodium, 20 g carbohydrates, 2 g fiber, 8 protein, 156 mg calcium, 2 mg iron

Wilted Spinach & Prosciutto Salad

Preparation time: 20 minutes
Cooking time: About 5 minutes

- ⅔ cup (about 1⅓ oz./ 38 g) dried tomatoes (not packed in oil)
- 1 jar (about 6 oz./ 170 g) marinated artichoke hearts
- 3 green onions
- 1 package (about 10 oz./ 285 g) prewashed spinach leaves, coarse stems and any yellow or bruised leaves discarded, remaining leaves rinsed and crisped
- ½ teaspoon olive oil
- 2 ounces (55 g) thinly sliced prosciutto, chopped
- 2 cloves garlic, minced
- ½ teaspoon dried rosemary
- 1 can (about 14 oz./ 400 g) artichoke hearts packed in water, drained and quartered
- ¼ cup (60 ml) balsamic vinegar
- 1 to 2 tablespoons firmly packed brown sugar

1. Place tomatoes in a small bowl and add boiling water to cover. Let stand until soft (about 10 minutes), stirring occasionally. Drain well; gently squeeze out excess liquid. Cut tomatoes into thin slivers; set aside.

2. While tomatoes are soaking, drain marinated artichokes, reserving marinade. Cut artichoke pieces lengthwise into halves; set aside. Cut onions into 2-inch (5-cm) lengths; then sliver each piece lengthwise. Tear spinach into bite-size pieces. Place onions and spinach in a large bowl; set aside.

3. Heat oil in a wide nonstick frying pan over medium-high heat. Add prosciutto, garlic, and rosemary. Cook, stirring often, until prosciutto is crisp and lightly browned (about 3 minutes); add water, 1 tablespoon (15 ml) at a time, if pan appears dry.

4. To pan, add tomatoes, marinated artichokes, artichoke marinade, quartered canned artichokes, vinegar, and sugar. Mix gently, stirring to scrape browned bits free from pan bottom. Pour artichoke mixture over spinach mixture; toss until spinach is slightly wilted and coated with dressing. Serve at once. Makes 4 servings.

Per serving: 170 calories (29% calories from fat), 6 g total fat, 1 g saturated fat, 11 mg cholesterol, 536 mg sodium, 22 g carbohydrates, 4 g fiber, 10 g protein, 92 mg calcium, 3 mg iron

Autumn Pear Salad

Preparation time: 20 minutes

- ¼ cup (60 ml) red wine vinegar
- 2 tablespoons (30 ml) extra-virgin olive oil
- 1 tablespoon drained capers
- 1 tablespoon (15 ml) lemon juice
- ¼ teaspoon *each* pepper and honey
- 4 large firm-ripe red pears (about 2 lbs./905 g *total*)
- 1 package (about 10 oz./285 g) pre-washed spinach leaves, coarse stems and any yellow or bruised leaves discarded, remaining leaves rinsed and crisped
- 8 ounces (230 g) mushrooms, thinly sliced
- ¾ cup (68 g) dried cranberries
- 4 ounces (115 g) sliced pancetta or bacon, crisply cooked, drained, and crumbled

1. In a large bowl, combine vinegar, oil, capers, lemon juice, pepper, and honey; beat until well blended. Set aside.

2. Core pears and cut each into about 16 wedges. As pears are cut, transfer them to bowl with dressing; mix gently to coat with dressing. Add spinach, mushrooms, and cranberries; mix until coated with dressing. Then divide salad among individual plates and sprinkle with pancetta. Makes 8 servings.

Per serving: 160 calories (29% calories from fat), 6 g total fat, 1 g saturated fat, 5 mg cholesterol, 163 mg sodium, 27 g carbohydrates, 4 g fiber, 3 g protein, 39 mg calcium, 1 mg iron

Melon, Basil & Bacon Salad

Preparation time: 25 minutes
Cooking time: About 20 minutes

- 6 ounces (170 g) sliced bacon
- 1½ tablespoons firmly packed brown sugar
- 8 cups (1.4 kg) peeled, seeded melon wedges (*each* about ¾ inch by 2 inches/2 cm by 5 cm); use any soft, aromatic melon, such as honeydew, cantaloupe, and/or crenshaw
- ¼ cup (60 ml) lime juice
- ⅓ cup (15 g) finely slivered fresh basil
  Basil sprigs

1. Line a shallow 10- by 15-inch (25- by 38-cm) baking pan with foil. Arrange bacon in pan in a single layer; bake in a 350°F (175°C) oven for 10 minutes. Spoon off and discard drippings. Evenly pat sugar onto bacon; bake until bacon is deep golden (about 10 more minutes).

2. Lift bacon to a board; let cool slightly, then cut diagonally into ½-inch (1-cm) slices. In a large, shallow bowl, combine melon, lime juice, and slivered basil. Top with bacon; garnish with basil sprigs. Makes 4 servings.

Per serving: 210 calories (26% calories from fat), 7 g total fat, 2 g saturated fat, 10 mg cholesterol, 226 mg sodium, 36 g carbohydrates, 3 g fiber, 6 g protein, 66 mg calcium, 1 mg iron

Fennel & Orange Salad

Preparation time: 20 minutes

- 2 large heads fennel (about 1½ lbs./680 g *total*)
- ¼ cup (60 ml) seasoned rice vinegar
- 2 tablespoons (30 ml) olive oil
- 1 tablespoon grated orange peel
- 1 teaspoon anise seeds
- 4 large oranges (about 2½ lbs./1.15 kg *total*)
  Seeds from 1 pomegranate (about 3½ inches/8.5 cm in diameter)
  Salt

1. Trim stems from fennel, reserving the feathery green leaves. Trim and discard any bruised areas from fennel; then cut each fennel head into thin slivers. Place slivered fennel in a large bowl.

2. Finely chop enough of the fennel leaves to make 1 tablespoon (reserve remaining leaves); add to bowl along with vinegar, oil, orange peel, and anise seeds. Mix well.

3. Cut off and discard peel and all white membrane from oranges. Cut fruit crosswise into slices about ¼ inch (6 mm) thick; discard seeds.

4. Divide fennel mixture among individual plates. Arrange oranges alongside fennel mixture; sprinkle salads equally with pomegranate seeds. Garnish with reserved fennel leaves. Season to taste with salt. Makes 6 servings.

Per serving: 147 calories (29% calories from fat), 5 g total fat, 0.6 g saturated fat, 0 mg cholesterol, 290 mg sodium, 26 g carbohydrates, 4 g fiber, 2 g protein, 110 mg calcium, 1 mg iron

Fig-stuffed Turkey Roast
(recipe on page 32)

Poultry & Seafood

Poultry and seafood have long been staples on Italian dinner tables. Naturally lean and compatible with all sorts of sauces and seasonings, these foods are perfect choices for low-fat entrées. This chapter includes a tempting selection of recipes, some simple, some elegant. For casual meals, try Fish & Fennel Stew or baked Lemon Rosemary Chicken; for dressier occasions, serve impressive Fig-stuffed Turkey Roast or Tuna Steaks with Roasted Peppers & Tuna Sauce.

•

Fig-stuffed Turkey Roast

Preparation time: 15 minutes
Cooking time: About 1¼ hours
Pictured on page 30

Stuffed with figs and seasoned with rosemary and mustard, this turkey roast makes a showy entrée.

1 turkey breast half (about 3½ lbs./1.6 kg), boned and skinned

3 tablespoons (45 ml) Dijon mustard

1 tablespoon chopped fresh rosemary or 1 teaspoon dried rosemary

12 dried Calimyrna or Mission figs, finely chopped

1 tablespoon (15 ml) honey

1 tablespoon (15 ml) olive oil

2 cloves garlic, minced

Pepper

Rosemary sprigs

1. Rinse turkey and pat dry. Then slice lengthwise down middle, cutting meat almost but not quite through. Push cut open and press turkey to make it lie as flat as possible. Spread turkey with mustard and sprinkle with half the chopped rosemary; set aside.

2. In a bowl, mix figs with honey. Mound fig mixture evenly down center of turkey. Starting from a long side, lift turkey and roll over filling to enclose. Tie roll snugly with cotton string at 2- to 3-inch (5- to 8-cm) intervals. Rub roll with oil, then with garlic; pat remaining chopped rosemary onto roll and sprinkle generously with pepper.

3. Place roll on a rack in a 9- by 13-inch (23- by 33-cm) baking pan; add ⅓ cup (80 ml) water to pan. Bake in a 375°F (190°C) oven until a meat thermometer inserted in thickest part of roll (insert thermometer in meat, not filling) registers 160° to 165°F (71° to 74°C), about 1¼ hours. Add water, ¼ cup (60 ml) at a time, if pan appears dry.

4. Remove roll from oven and let stand for 10 minutes; then snip and discard strings and cut roll crosswise into thick slices. Garnish with rosemary sprigs. Serve with pan juices, if desired. Makes 6 to 8 servings.

Per serving: 308 calories (10% calories from fat), 3 g total fat, 0.7 g saturated fat, 117 mg cholesterol, 232 mg sodium, 24 g carbohydrates, 3 g fiber, 44 g protein, 67 mg calcium, 3 mg iron

Sautéed Turkey with Provolone & Sage

Preparation time: 15 minutes
Cooking time: About 5 minutes

When time is short, try thin-sliced, sautéed turkey breast topped with cheese and aromatic fresh sage.

1 pound (455 g) thinly sliced turkey breast

2 teaspoons finely chopped fresh sage or 1 teaspoon dried sage

2 teaspoons olive oil

⅓ cup (45 g) finely shredded provolone or part-skim mozzarella cheese

Pepper

Sage sprigs

Lemon wedges

Salt

1. Rinse turkey and pat dry. Sprinkle one side of each slice with chopped sage; set aside.

2. Heat 1 teaspoon of the oil in a wide nonstick frying pan over medium-high heat. Add half the turkey, sage-coated side down, and cook until golden on bottom (about 1½ minutes). Then turn pieces over and continue to cook until no longer pink in center; cut to test (30 to 60 more seconds). Transfer cooked turkey to a platter and sprinkle with half the cheese. Cover loosely with foil and keep warm.

3. Immediately cook remaining turkey, using remaining 1 teaspoon oil; add water, 1 tablespoon (15 ml) at a time, if pan appears dry. Transfer turkey to platter.

4. Sprinkle turkey with remaining cheese, then with pepper; garnish with sage sprigs. Serve at once. Season to taste with lemon and salt. Makes 4 servings.

Per serving: 184 calories (30% calories from fat), 6 g total fat, 2 g saturated fat, 78 mg cholesterol, 149 mg sodium, 0.3 g carbohydrates, 0 g fiber, 31 g protein, 94 mg calcium, 1 mg iron

To give tender turkey slices an intriguing flavor, "cure" them briefly in salt and sugar; then rub the meat with herbs and garlic before sautéing.

1 tablespoon salt

1½ teaspoons sugar

1½ pounds (680 g) thinly sliced turkey breast

¼ cup (25 g) sliced green onions

2 tablespoons finely chopped Italian or regular parsley

3 cloves garlic, minced

1 teaspoon chopped fresh oregano or ½ teaspoon dried oregano

½ teaspoon *each* coarsely ground pepper and grated lemon peel

2 teaspoons olive oil

Italian or regular parsley sprigs

Lemon wedges

Oregano-rubbed Turkey

Preparation time: 15 minutes
Marinating time: At least 2 hours
Cooking time: About 5 minutes

1. In a large bowl, combine salt and sugar. Rinse turkey and pat dry; then add to bowl and turn to coat evenly with salt mixture. Cover and refrigerate for at least 2 hours or up to 3 hours. Rinse turkey well, drain, and pat dry.

2. In a small bowl, combine onions, chopped parsley, garlic, oregano, pepper, and lemon peel. Rub onion mixture evenly over both sides of each turkey slice.

3. Heat 1 teaspoon of the oil in a wide nonstick frying pan over medium-high heat. Add half the turkey and cook until golden on bottom (about 1½ minutes). Then turn pieces over and continue to cook until no longer pink in center; cut to test (30 to 60 more seconds). Transfer cooked turkey to a platter, cover loosely with foil, and keep warm.

4. Immediately cook remaining turkey, using remaining 1 teaspoon oil; add water, 1 tablespoon (15 ml) at a time, if pan appears dry. Transfer turkey to platter and garnish with parsley sprigs. Serve at once. Season to taste with lemon. Makes 6 servings.

Per serving: 148 calories (14% calories from fat), 2 g total fat, 0.4 g saturated fat, 70 mg cholesterol, 1,155 mg sodium, 2 g carbohydrates, 0.2 g fiber, 28 g protein, 29 mg calcium, 2 mg iron

---

Crisp bread crumbs coat these moist, lemon-seasoned chicken breasts.

6 boneless, skinless chicken breast halves (about 2¼ lbs./1.1 kg *total*)

1¼ cups (38 g) soft whole wheat bread crumbs

2 tablespoons chopped fresh rosemary or 2 teaspoons dried rosemary

1 tablespoon chopped Italian or regular parsley

1 teaspoon grated lemon peel

½ teaspoon pepper

1 tablespoon (15 ml) lemon juice

Lemon wedges

Salt

Lemon Rosemary Chicken

Preparation time: 15 minutes
Cooking time: About 25 minutes

1. Rinse chicken and pat dry; then arrange, skinned side up, in an oiled shallow 10- by 15-inch (25- by 38-cm) baking pan. Set aside.

2. In a small bowl, mix bread crumbs, rosemary, parsley, lemon peel, and pepper. Moisten top of each chicken piece with lemon juice; press crumb mixture equally over each piece, covering evenly.

3. Bake in a 400°F (205°C) oven until crumb coating is browned and meat in thickest part is no longer pink; cut to test (about 25 minutes). Season chicken to taste with lemon and salt. Makes 6 servings.

Per serving: 185 calories (11% calories from fat), 2 g total fat, 0.5 g saturated fat, 88 mg cholesterol, 133 mg sodium, 3 g carbohydrates, 0.5 g fiber, 36 g protein, 28 mg calcium, 1 mg iron

Just right for special occasions, these split and roasted game hens are served on a bed of saffron-tinted orzo.

....

2 **Rock Cornish game hens (about 1½ lbs./680 g *each*)**

¼ **cup (60 ml) dry white wine or apple juice**

2 **tablespoons (30 ml) *each* Dijon mustard and honey**

1 **tablespoon chopped fresh thyme or 1 teaspoon dried thyme**

3⅓ **cups (790 ml) fat-free reduced-sodium chicken broth**

Large pinch of saffron threads or ⅛ teaspoon ground saffron (or to taste)

1¼ **cups (285 g) dried orzo or other tiny rice-shaped pasta**

¼ **cup (25 g) thinly sliced green onions**

Thyme sprigs

Salt and pepper

Herb-roasted Game Hens with Saffron Orzo

....

Preparation time: 20 minutes
Cooking time: About 25 minutes
Pictured on facing page

1. Reserve game hen necks and giblets for other uses. With poultry shears or a sharp knife, split each hen in half, cutting along backbone and breastbone. Rinse hens and pat dry. In a medium-size bowl, mix wine, mustard, honey, and chopped thyme. Dip hens in marinade and turn to coat; then lift out and drain briefly, reserving marinade. Place hens, skin side up, on a rack in a foil-lined 12- by 15-inch (30- by 38-cm) broiler pan.

2. Bake hens in bottom third of a 425°F (220°C) oven until meat near thighbone is no longer pink; cut to test (about 25 minutes). Halfway through cooking, brush hens with marinade.

3. While hens are baking, bring broth and saffron to a boil in a 2- to 3-quart (1.9- to 2.8-liter) pan over high heat. Stir in pasta. Reduce heat, cover, and simmer, stirring occasionally, until almost all liquid has been absorbed (about 15 minutes); as liquid cooks down, stir more often and watch closely to prevent scorching.

4. Stir onions into pasta; then divide pasta mixture among 4 individual rimmed plates. Place one hen half on each plate; garnish with thyme sprigs. Season to taste with salt and pepper. Makes 4 servings.

....

Per serving: 688 calories (29% calories from fat), 21 g total fat, 6 g saturated fat, 132 mg cholesterol, 847 mg sodium, 63 g carbohydrates, 2 g fiber, 53 g protein, 48 mg calcium, 5 mg iron

Herb-roasted Game Hens with
Saffron Orzo
(recipe on facing page)

Roasted Garlic

White Bean & Roasted Garlic Bruschetta

Preparation time: 20 minutes
Cooking time: About 1¼ hours

· ·

- 1 **large head garlic (about 4 oz./115 g)**
- ½ **teaspoon olive oil**
- 8 **slices crusty bread, such as Italian ciabatta or sourdough (*each* about ½ inch/1 cm thick; about 8 oz./ 230 g *total*)**
- 2 **cans (about 15 oz./ 425 g *each*) cannellini (white kidney beans)**
- ½ **cup (20 g) lightly packed fresh basil leaves**
- ¼ **cup (15 g) chopped Italian or regular parsley**
- ¼ **cup (60 ml) lemon juice**
- 4 **teaspoons (20 ml) Oriental sesame oil**
- ½ **teaspoon salt**
- 1 **pound (455 g) pear-shaped (Roma-type) tomatoes, thinly sliced**
- 4 **to 6 teaspoons drained capers (or to taste)**
  Fresh basil leaves
  About 12 canned mild cherry peppers, drained (optional)
  Pepper

· ·

1. Slice ¼ inch (6 mm) off top of garlic head. Then rub garlic with olive oil. Wrap garlic in foil and bake in a 375°F (190°C)

oven until soft when pressed (about 1¼ hours). Carefully remove garlic from foil; transfer to a rack and let stand until cool enough to touch (about 10 minutes).

2. Meanwhile, arrange bread slices slightly apart in a large, shallow baking pan. Broil about 6 inches below heat, turning once, until golden on both sides (about 5 minutes). Let cool on a rack.

3. Squeeze garlic cloves from skins into a food processor or blender. Drain beans, reserving liquid. Rinse beans and add to processor along with the ½ cup (20 g) basil leaves, parsley, lemon juice, sesame oil, and salt. Whirl until coarsely puréed. If necessary, add enough of the reserved bean liquid to make mixture spreadable (do not make it too thin). Discard remaining liquid.

4. Top toast slices equally with bean mixture; arrange tomato slices, capers, and basil leaves over bean mixture. Serve with cherry peppers, if desired. Season to taste with pepper. Makes 4 servings.

Per serving: 445 calories (16% calories from fat), 8 g total fat, 1 g saturated fat, 0 mg cholesterol, 1,455 mg sodium, 77 g carbohydrates, 17 g fiber, 19 g protein, 233 mg calcium, 7 mg iron

Garlic Mashed Potatoes

Preparation time: 20 minutes
Cooking time: About 35 minutes

· ·

- 1 **tablespoon (15 ml) olive oil**
- 3 **or 4 medium-size heads garlic (9 to 12 oz./ 255 to 340 g *total*)**
- 4 **pounds (1.8 kg) russet potatoes**
- 1 **large package (about 8 oz./230 g) Neufchâtel cheese, at room temperature**
- ¾ **to 1 cup (180 to 240 ml) fat-free reduced-sodium chicken broth**
  Salt

· ·

1. Pour oil into a shallow baking pan. Cut garlic heads in half crosswise through cloves; place, cut side down, in pan. Bake in a 375°F (190°C) oven until cut side is golden brown (about 35 minutes). Using a thin spatula, lift garlic from pan and transfer to a rack; let stand until cool enough to touch (about 10 minutes).

2. While garlic is baking, peel potatoes and cut into 2-inch (5-cm) chunks; place in a 5- to 6-quart (5- to 6-liter) pan and add enough water to cover. Bring to a boil over medium-high heat; reduce heat, cover, and boil gently until potatoes mash very easily when pressed

(25 to 30 minutes). Drain potatoes well; transfer to a large bowl and keep warm.

3. Reserve 1 or 2 half-heads of garlic. Squeeze cloves from remaining garlic; add to potatoes along with Neufchâtel cheese. Mash potatoes with a potato masher or an electric mixer, adding broth as needed to make potatoes as soft and creamy as desired. Season to taste with salt and swirl into a shallow serving dish. Garnish with reserved roasted garlic. Makes 8 servings.

Per serving: 304 calories (26% calories from fat), 9 g total fat, 4 g saturated fat, 22 mg cholesterol, 205 mg sodium, 48 g carbohydrates, 4 g fiber, 9 g protein, 80 mg calcium, 2 mg iron

Roasted Green Beans & Garlic

Preparation time: 15 minutes
Cooking time: About 1 hour

· ·

- 1 **medium-size head garlic (3 oz./85 g)**
- 1½ **teaspoons olive oil**
- 1½ **pounds (680 g) slender green beans, ends trimmed**
- 1 **ounce (30 g) thinly sliced prosciutto, coarsely chopped**
  Pepper

· ·

1. Slice ¼ inch (6 mm) off top of garlic head. Then rub garlic with ½ teaspoon of the oil. Wrap garlic in foil; set aside. In a shallow 10- by 15-inch (25- by 38-cm) baking pan, combine beans and remaining 1 teaspoon oil.

2. Bake foil-wrapped garlic (on oven rack) and beans in a 375°F (190°C) oven until garlic is very soft when pressed (about 1 hour) and ends of beans are tinged with brown (about 50 minutes; add water, ¼ cup/60 ml at a time, if pan appears dry).

3. Carefully remove garlic from foil; transfer to a rack and let stand until cool enough to touch (about 10 minutes). Gently squeeze or pry garlic cloves from skins (try not to smash cloves). Sprinkle garlic and prosciutto over beans. Return to oven and bake just until prosciutto is tinged with brown (2 to 5 minutes). Season to taste with pepper. Makes 4 to 6 servings.

Per serving: 105 calories (26% calories from fat), 3 g total fat, 0.5 g saturated fat, 5 mg cholesterol, 116 mg sodium, 16 g carbohydrates, 3 g fiber, 5 g protein, 86 mg calcium, 2 mg iron

Garlic Chicken

Preparation time: 15 minutes
Cooking time: About 1½ hours

- 1 **large head garlic (about 4 oz./115 g)**
- ½ **teaspoon olive oil**
- 4 **boneless, skinless chicken breast halves (1½ lbs./680 g *total*)**
- 1 **tablespoon chopped fresh thyme or 1 teaspoon dried thyme**
- ¼ **teaspoon coarsely ground pepper**
- ⅛ **teaspoon salt**
- ¼ **cup (28 g) shredded fontina cheese**
- 4 **small thyme sprigs**

1. Slice ¼ inch (6 mm) off top of garlic head. Then rub garlic with oil. Wrap garlic in foil and bake in a 375°F (190°C) oven until very soft when pressed (about 1¼ hours). Carefully remove garlic from foil; transfer to a rack and let stand until cool enough to touch (about 10 minutes).

2. Meanwhile, rinse chicken, pat dry, and sprinkle with chopped thyme and pepper. Place, skinned side up, in a lightly oiled 9-inch (23-cm) baking pan. Bake in a 450°F (230°C) oven until meat in thickest part is no longer pink; cut to test (12 to 15 minutes). Meanwhile, squeeze garlic cloves from skins into a small bowl. Add salt; mash garlic thoroughly with a fork, incorporating salt.

3. Spread a fourth of the garlic mixture over each chicken piece; then sprinkle chicken with cheese. Return to oven; continue to bake just until cheese is melted and bubbly (about 3 more minutes). Press a thyme sprig into cheese on each piece of chicken. Makes 4 servings.

Per serving: 258 calories (18% calories from fat), 5 g total fat, 2 g saturated fat, 107 mg cholesterol, 241 mg sodium, 9 g carbohydrates, 0.5 g fiber, 43 g protein, 112 mg calcium, 2 mg iron

Roasted Garlic Flatbread

Preparation time: 15 minutes
Cooking time: About 1½ hours

- 1 **medium-size head garlic (3 oz./85 g)**
- ¼ **cup (60 ml) olive oil**
- 2 **cups (250 g) all-purpose flour**
- 4 **teaspoons baking powder**
- 1½ **teaspoons sugar**
- ¼ **to ½ teaspoon *each* pepper and salt**
- ¾ **cup (180 ml) nonfat milk**
- ¼ **cup (35 g) yellow cornmeal**
- 1 **large egg white beaten with 1 teaspoon water**
- ½ **teaspoon dried rosemary**
- ⅛ **teaspoon coarsely ground pepper**

1. Roast and cool garlic as directed for Garlic Chicken (at left), using ½ teaspoon of the oil, but roast for only 1 hour. When garlic is cool, squeeze cloves from skins into a small bowl; add remaining oil. Mash garlic thoroughly with a fork, mixing it with oil.

2. In a large bowl, stir together flour, baking powder, sugar, the ¼ to ½ teaspoon pepper, and salt. Add milk and garlic-oil mixture; stir just until dry ingredients are evenly moistened. In bowl, knead dough a few turns with lightly floured fingers.

3. Sprinkle cornmeal over bottom of an 8-inch-square (20-cm-square) nonstick baking pan. Scrape dough into pan and pat it evenly over pan bottom. With your fingers, poke holes liberally in surface of dough. Brush dough with egg white mixture; sprinkle with rosemary and the coarsely ground pepper.

4. Bake in a 400°F (205°C) oven until bread is a rich brown (20 to 25 minutes). Let stand for 3 to 5 minutes; then cut into squares. Serve hot or warm. Makes 6 servings.

Per serving: 291 calories (30% calories from fat), 10 g total fat, 1 g saturated fat, 0.6 mg cholesterol, 441 mg sodium, 44 g carbohydrates, 2 g fiber, 7 g protein, 250 mg calcium, 3 mg iron

Salt-grilled Shrimp
(recipe on facing page)

A honey-sweetened red onion marmalade dresses up these simple baked chicken breasts.

- 6 small boneless, skinless chicken breast halves (1½ to 1¾ lbs./680 to 795 g *total*)
- 3 tablespoons (45 ml) cream sherry
- 2 small red onions (about 6 oz./170 g *each*)
- ½ cup (120 ml) dry red wine
- 1 tablespoon (15 ml) *each* red wine vinegar and honey

  Italian or regular parsley sprigs

  Salt and pepper

1. Rinse chicken, pat dry, and place in a heavy-duty plastic food-storage bag; add 2 tablespoons (30 ml) of

Sherried Chicken with Onion Marmalade

Preparation time: 15 minutes
Marinating time: At least 30 minutes
Cooking time: About 20 minutes

the sherry. Seal bag and rotate to coat chicken with sherry. Refrigerate for at least 30 minutes or up to 6 hours, turning bag over several times.

2. Thinly slice onions; wrap several slices airtight and refrigerate. In a wide frying pan, combine remaining onion slices, wine, vinegar, and honey. Cook over medium-high

heat, stirring often, until liquid has evaporated. Remove from heat and stir in remaining 1 tablespoon (15 ml) sherry. Set aside.

3. Turn chicken and its marinade into a 9- by 13-inch (23- by 33-cm) baking pan; arrange chicken, skinned side up, in a single layer. Bake in a 450°F (230°C) oven until meat in thickest part is no longer pink; cut to test (12 to 15 minutes). With a slotted spoon, transfer chicken to a platter. Top with onion mixture. Garnish with reserved onion slices and parsley sprigs. Season to taste with salt and pepper. Makes 6 servings.

Per serving: 200 calories (9% calories from fat), 2 g total fat, 0.4 g saturated fat, 74 mg cholesterol, 91 mg sodium, 9 g carbohydrates, 0.9 g fiber, 30 g protein, 33 mg calcium, 1 mg iron

---

Smoky grilled shrimp are served with a salad of crisp greens and tiny tomatoes for a quick and appealing main course.

- 1½ pounds (680 g) extra-jumbo raw shrimp (16 to 20 per lb.)

  About 2 tablespoons sea salt or kosher salt

- 5 to 6 ounces (140 to 170 g) Belgian endive, separated into leaves, rinsed, and crisped
- 8 ounces (230 g) small romaine lettuce leaves, rinsed and crisped
- 12 ounces (340 g) tiny red and/ or yellow cherry tomatoes

  About ½ cup (120 ml) balsamic vinegar

- 1 tablespoon (15 ml) extra-virgin olive oil

  Pepper

Salt-grilled Shrimp

Preparation time: 25 minutes
Cooking time: About 8 minutes
Pictured on facing page

1. Insert a wooden pick under back of each shrimp between shell segments; gently pull up to remove vein. If vein breaks, repeat in another place. Rinse and drain deveined shrimp; then roll in salt to coat lightly.

2. Mix endive, lettuce, and tomatoes in a large bowl.

3. Place shrimp on a lightly greased grill 4 to 6 inches (10 to 15 cm) above a solid bed of hot coals.

Cook, turning once, until shrimp are just opaque in center; cut to test (about 8 minutes). Meanwhile, divide salad among individual plates.

4. To serve, arrange shrimp atop salads. To eat, shell shrimp and season to taste with vinegar, oil, and pepper. Makes 4 servings.

Per serving: 213 calories (27% calories from fat), 6 g total fat, 1 g saturated fat, 210 mg cholesterol, 1,325 mg sodium, 9 g carbohydrates, 3 g fiber, 30 g protein, 104 mg calcium, 5 mg iron

Lightly battered and sautéed, plump shrimp sprinkled with capers make a great main dish.

- 3 or 4 large lemons, thinly sliced
- 2 large egg whites
- ¾ cup (96 g) cornstarch
- ¼ cup (25 g) fine dry bread crumbs
- 1 teaspoon baking powder
- ¼ teaspoon salt
- 1 tablespoon butter or margarine
- 1 tablespoon (15 ml) olive oil
- 1 pound (455 g) large raw shrimp (31 to 35 per lb.), shelled and deveined
- ¼ teaspoon grated lemon peel
- 1 to 2 tablespoons drained capers (or to taste)

Sautéed Lemon-Caper Shrimp

Preparation time: 25 minutes
Cooking time: About 5 minutes

1. Arrange lemon slices on a rimmed platter; cover and set aside.

2. In a large bowl, beat egg whites and ⅓ cup (80 ml) water until blended. Add cornstarch, bread crumbs, baking powder, and salt; stir until smooth.

3. Melt butter in oil in a wide non-stick frying pan over medium-high heat. Meanwhile, dip shrimp in batter. Lift out and drain briefly to let excess batter drip off; discard remaining batter.

4. When butter-oil mixture is hot, add shrimp to pan; sprinkle shrimp with lemon peel. Cook, separating shrimp and turning gently, until shrimp are lightly browned on outside and just opaque in center; cut to test (about 4 minutes). Arrange shrimp over lemon slices on platter and sprinkle with capers. Makes 4 servings.

Per serving: 303 calories (23% calories from fat), 9 g total fat, 3 g saturated fat, 147 mg cholesterol, 596 mg sodium, 41 g carbohydrates, 0.5 g fiber, 23 g protein, 206 mg calcium, 4 mg iron

---

Robust yet light, this traditional Italian favorite goes together in less than an hour.

- 2 cans (about 6½ oz./185 g *each*) chopped clams
- 1 teaspoon olive oil
- 2 cloves garlic, minced
- 1 can (about 15 oz./425 g) tomato purée
- 2 tablespoons chopped fresh basil or 1 tablespoon dried basil
- 8 ounces (230 g) dried linguine
- 1 large tomato (about 8 oz./ 230 g), finely chopped
- ¼ cup (20 g) grated Parmesan cheese
  Basil sprigs
  Crushed red pepper flakes

1. Drain clams, reserving liquid; set clams and liquid aside.

Linguine with Tomato-Clam Sauce

Preparation time: 15 minutes
Cooking time: About 25 minutes

2. Heat oil in a 3- to 4-quart (2.8- to 3.8-liter) pan over medium heat. Add garlic and cook, stirring, just until fragrant (about 30 seconds; do not scorch). Add clam liquid, tomato purée, and chopped basil. Bring to a boil over high heat; then reduce heat and simmer, uncovered, until reduced to 2 cups (470 ml), about 20 minutes. Stir often to prevent scorching, scraping bottom of pan as you stir.

3. While sauce is simmering, cook pasta. In a 4- to 5-quart (3.8- to 5-liter) pan, bring about 8 cups (1.9 liters) water to a boil over medium-high heat; stir in pasta and cook until just tender to bite, 8 to 10 minutes. (Or cook pasta according to package directions.) Drain well, transfer to a large serving bowl, and keep warm.

4. Add clams and chopped tomato to sauce; stir just until heated through. Spoon sauce over pasta and sprinkle with cheese. Garnish with basil sprigs. Season to taste with red pepper flakes. Makes 4 servings.

Per serving: 380 calories (12% calories from fat), 5 g total fat, 2 g saturated fat, 37 mg cholesterol, 601 mg sodium, 59 g carbohydrates, 5 g fiber, 25 g protein, 189 mg calcium, 17 mg iron

Succulent scallops and pasta seashells in a simple wine-cheese sauce are delightful for casual company gatherings or family meals.

2 ounces (55 g) Neufchâtel or cream cheese, at room temperature

2 teaspoons honey

1 teaspoon Dijon mustard

½ teaspoon grated lemon peel

1 pound (455 g) sea scallops

8 ounces (230 g) dried medium-size pasta shells

¾ cup (180 ml) fat-free reduced-sodium chicken broth

¼ cup (15 g) finely chopped Italian or regular parsley

2 teaspoons dry white wine (or to taste)

¼ cup (20 g) grated Parmesan cheese

Scallops & Shells with Lemon Cream

Preparation time: 20 minutes
Cooking time: About 15 minutes

1. In a food processor or blender, whirl Neufchâtel cheese, honey, mustard, and lemon peel until smooth; set aside. Rinse scallops and pat dry; cut into bite-size pieces, if desired. Set aside.

2. In a 4- to 5-quart (3.8- to 5-liter) pan, bring about 8 cups (1.9 liters) water to a boil over medium-high heat; stir in pasta and cook until just tender to bite, 8 to 10 minutes. (Or cook pasta according to package directions.) Drain well, transfer to a large serving bowl, and keep warm.

3. In a 3- to 4-quart (2.8- to 3.8-liter) pan, bring broth to a boil over high heat. Add scallops and cook until just opaque in center; cut to test (1 to 2 minutes).

4. With a slotted spoon, transfer scallops to bowl with pasta; keep warm. Quickly pour scallop cooking liquid from pan into Neufchâtel cheese mixture in food processor; whirl until smooth. With a spoon, stir in parsley and wine. Pour sauce over scallops and pasta; sprinkle with Parmesan cheese. Serve immediately. Makes 4 servings.

Per serving: 393 calories (16% calories from fat), 7 g total fat, 3 g saturated fat, 53 mg cholesterol, 509 mg sodium, 49 g carbohydrates, 2 g fiber, 31 g protein, 138 mg calcium, 3 mg iron

Pink peppercorns poached to softness add an attractive color and a delicately spicy flavor to baked swordfish steaks.

Pink Peppercorn Swordfish

Preparation time: 15 minutes
Cooking time: About 15 minutes
Pictured on facing page

⅓ cup (21 g) whole pink peppercorns

4 swordfish or halibut steaks (*each* about 1 inch/2.5 cm thick and 5 to 6 oz./140 to 170 g)

8 teaspoons (40 ml) honey

4 large butter lettuce leaves, rinsed and crisped

2 jars (about 6 oz./170 g *each*) marinated artichoke hearts, drained

Lemon wedges

1. In a 1- to 1½-quart (950-ml to 1.4-liter) pan, combine peppercorns and about 2 cups (470 ml) water. Bring to a boil over high heat; then reduce heat and simmer until peppercorns are slightly softened (about 4 minutes). Drain well.

2. Rinse fish and pat dry. Arrange pieces well apart in a lightly oiled shallow 10- by 15-inch (25- by 38-cm) baking pan. Brush each piece with 2 teaspoons of the honey; then top equally with peppercorns, spreading them in a single layer.

3. Bake in a 400°F (205°C) oven until fish is just opaque but still moist in thickest part; cut to test (about 10 minutes).

4. Place one lettuce leaf on each of 4 individual plates; top lettuce with artichokes. With a wide spatula, lift fish from baking pan and arrange alongside lettuce. Season to taste with lemon. Makes 4 servings.

Per serving: 277 calories (29% calories from fat), 9 g total fat, 2 g saturated fat, 54 mg cholesterol, 361 mg sodium, 21 g carbohydrates, 3 g fiber, 30 g protein, 44 mg calcium, 3 mg iron

---

Serve this bold seafood stew with plenty of crusty bread to soak up the flavorful broth.

Cioppino

Preparation time: 30 minutes
Cooking time: About 45 minutes

1 tablespoon (15 ml) olive oil

1 large onion, chopped

1 large red bell pepper (about 8 oz./230 g), seeded and chopped

⅓ cup (20 g) chopped Italian or regular parsley

2 cloves garlic, minced

4 or 5 large tomatoes (2 to 2½ lbs./905 g to 1.15 kg *total*), peeled and cut into chunks

1 large can (about 15 oz./425 g) tomato sauce

1 cup (240 ml) dry red wine

1 dried bay leaf

1 tablespoon chopped fresh basil or 1 teaspoon dried basil

2 teaspoons chopped fresh oregano or ½ teaspoon dried oregano

12 small hard-shell clams (suitable for steaming), scrubbed

1 pound (455 g) extra-jumbo raw shrimp (16 to 20 per lb.), shelled and deveined

1 pound (455 g) firm-textured, white-fleshed fish, such as rockfish, cut into 2-inch (5-cm) chunks

2 cooked whole Dungeness crabs (about 2 lbs./905 g *each*), cleaned and cracked

Salt

1. Heat oil in an 8- to 10-quart (8- to 10-liter) pan over medium-high heat. Add onion, bell pepper, parsley, garlic, and ¼ cup (60 ml) water. Cook, stirring often, until onion is soft (about 5 minutes); add water, 1 tablespoon (15 ml) at a time, if pan appears dry.

2. Stir in tomatoes, tomato sauce, wine, bay leaf, basil, and oregano. Bring to a boil; then reduce heat, cover, and simmer until flavors are blended (about 20 minutes).

3. Gently stir in clams, shrimp, fish, and crabs. Cover tightly and bring to a boil over high heat. Reduce heat and simmer gently until clams pop open and fish is just opaque but still moist in thickest part; cut to test (10 to 15 minutes).

4. Ladle stew into large soup bowls, discarding bay leaf and any unopened clams. Season to taste with salt. Makes 8 servings.

Per serving: 264 calories (18% calories from fat), 5 g total fat, 0.8 g saturated fat, 149 mg cholesterol, 597 mg sodium, 15 g carbohydrates, 3 g fiber, 35 g protein, 126 mg calcium, 5 mg iron

Pink Peppercorn Swordfish
(recipe on facing page)

Sliced fennel lends a refreshing anise flavor to this garlicky stew of fish and Roma tomatoes.

....

- 1 **large head fennel (about 12 oz./340 g)**
- 1 **tablespoon (15 ml) olive oil**
- 1 **large onion, chopped**
- 6 **cloves garlic, minced**
- 1¼ **pounds (565 g) pear-shaped (Roma-type) tomatoes, chopped**
- 2 **cups (470 ml) fat-free reduced-sodium chicken broth**
- 1 **bottle (about 8 oz./230 g) clam juice**
- ½ **cup (120 ml) dry white wine**
- ¼ **to ½ teaspoon ground red pepper (cayenne)**

Fish & Fennel Stew

....

Preparation time: 25 minutes
Cooking time: About 40 minutes

- 1½ **pounds (680 g) boneless, skinless firm-textured, light-fleshed fish, such as halibut, swordfish, or sea bass, cut into 1½-inch (3.5-cm) chunks**

....

1. Trim stems from fennel, reserving feathery green leaves. Trim and discard any bruised areas from fennel. Finely chop leaves and set aside; thinly slice fennel head.

2. Heat oil in a 5- to 6-quart (5- to 6-liter) pan over medium heat. Add sliced fennel, onion, and garlic; cook, stirring often, until onion is sweet tasting and all vegetables are browned (about 20 minutes). Add water, ¼ cup (60 ml) at a time, if pan appears dry.

3. Add tomatoes, broth, clam juice, wine, and red pepper. Bring to a boil; then reduce heat, cover, and simmer for 10 minutes. Add fish, cover, and simmer until just opaque but still moist in thickest part; cut to test (about 5 minutes). Stir in fennel leaves. Makes 4 servings.

....

Per serving: 317 calories (24% calories from fat), 8 g total fat, 1 g saturated fat, 54 mg cholesterol, 628 mg sodium, 16 g carbohydrates, 4 g fiber, 40 g protein, 151 mg calcium, 3 mg iron

---

Coarsely ground dried mushrooms make an unusual coating for baked salmon fillets. Serve the fish with fresh asparagus and whimsical pasta bow ties.

....

- ¼ **ounce/8 g (about ⅓ cup) dried porcini mushrooms**
- 2 **tablespoons fine dry bread crumbs**
- ¼ **teaspoon salt**
- 8 **ounces (230 g) dried farfalle (pasta bow ties)**
- 8 **ounces (230 g) asparagus, tough ends snapped off, spears cut diagonally into thin slices**
- 1 **to 1¼ pounds (455 to 565 g) boneless, skinless salmon fillet (1 inch/2.5 cm thick), cut into 4 equal pieces**
- 2 **tablespoons (30 ml) olive oil**

Porcini-crusted Salmon

....

Preparation time: 20 minutes
Cooking time: About 15 minutes

....

1. In a food processor or blender, whirl mushrooms to make a coarse powder. Add bread crumbs and salt; whirl to mix, then pour into a wide, shallow bowl. Set aside.

2. In a 5- to 6-quart (5- to 6-liter) pan, bring about 3 quarts (2.8 liters) water to a boil over medium-high heat. Stir in pasta and cook for 5 minutes; then add asparagus and cook, stirring occasionally, until pasta and asparagus are just tender to bite (3 to 5 more minutes).

3. While pasta is cooking, rinse fish and pat dry; then turn fish in mushroom mixture, pressing to coat well all over. Lay fish pieces, flatter side down and well apart, in a shallow 10- by 15-inch (25- by 38-cm) baking pan. Pat any remaining mushroom mixture on fish; drizzle evenly with oil. Bake in a 400°F (205°C) oven until fish is just opaque but still moist in thickest part; cut to test (about 10 minutes).

4. When pasta mixture is done, drain it well and divide among 4 shallow individual bowls; keep warm. With a wide spatula, lift fish from baking pan; set in bowls atop pasta. Drizzle pan juices over pasta and fish. Makes 4 servings.

....

Per serving: 483 calories (30% calories from fat), 16 g total fat, 2 g saturated fat, 71 mg cholesterol, 226 mg sodium, 48 g carbohydrates, 2 g fiber, 35 g protein, 48 mg calcium, 4 mg iron

Fresh tuna is delicious served rare—but if you use fish that has not been previously frozen, freeze it at 0°F (-18°C) for at least 7 days to destroy any potentially harmful organisms it may contain. Thaw the fish in the refrigerator before cooking.

- 5½ cups (1.3 liters) fat-free reduced-sodium chicken broth
- ½ cup (65 g) finely chopped dried apricots
- 1 pound (455 g) dried orzo or other tiny rice-shaped pasta
- 1 can (about 6⅛ oz./174 g) tuna packed in water
- 1 large egg yolk or 1 table-spoon (15 ml) pasteurized egg substitute
- ¼ teaspoon grated lemon peel
- 2 tablespoons (30 ml) lemon juice
- 4 teaspoons (20 ml) balsamic vinegar
- 1 teaspoon honey
- ½ teaspoon Dijon mustard
- ½ teaspoon salt (or to taste)
- ¼ cup (60 ml) *each* olive oil and salad oil
- 3 canned anchovy fillets, drained
- 1 cup (240 ml) nonfat sour cream
- 2 tablespoons fennel seeds
- 1 tablespoon whole white peppercorns
- 1½ teaspoons coriander seeds
- 2 large egg whites
- 4 tuna (ahi) steaks (*each* about 1 inch/2.5 cm thick and about 7 oz./200 g)
- 1 teaspoon olive oil

Tuna Steaks with Roasted Peppers & Tuna Sauce

Preparation time: 35 minutes
Cooking time: About 20 minutes

- ½ cup (120 ml) bottled clam juice
- 1 jar roasted red peppers (about 12 oz./340 g), drained and patted dry
- 3 tablespoons drained capers (or to taste)
- Lemon slices
- Italian or regular parsley sprigs

1. In a 4- to 5-quart (3.8- to 5-liter) pan, bring broth and apricots to a boil over high heat; stir in orzo. Reduce heat, cover, and simmer, stirring occasionally, until almost all liquid has been absorbed (about 20 minutes); as liquid cooks down, stir more often and watch closely to prevent scorching. Remove from heat and keep warm.

2. While orzo is cooking, drain can of tuna, reserving ¼ cup (60 ml) of the liquid from can. Set tuna and liquid aside.

3. In a food processor or blender, combine egg yolk, lemon peel, lemon juice, vinegar, honey, mustard, and ¼ teaspoon of the salt (or to taste); whirl until blended. With motor running, slowly pour in the ¼ cup (60 ml) olive oil and salad oil in a thin, steady stream. Whirl until

well blended. Add canned tuna, reserved tuna liquid, 1 tablespoon (15 ml) water, and anchovies; whirl until smoothly puréed. With a spoon or whisk, stir in sour cream; set aside.

4. Wash and dry food processor or blender; then combine fennel seeds, peppercorns, coriander seeds, and remaining ¼ teaspoon salt in processor or blender. Whirl until finely ground; transfer to a wide, shallow bowl. In another wide, shallow bowl, beat egg whites to blend. Rinse tuna steaks and pat dry; then cut each in half. Dip pieces, one at a time, in egg whites; drain briefly, then coat on both sides with seed mixture. Pat any remaining seed mixture on fish.

5. Heat the 1 teaspoon olive oil in a wide nonstick frying pan over medium-high heat. Add fish and cook, turning once, until browned on both sides. Add clam juice. Reduce heat and cook until fish is still pale pink in center; cut to test (about 5 minutes).

6. Spoon pasta onto a rimmed plat-ter; fluff with a fork. With a slotted spoon, lift fish from pan and place atop pasta; arrange red peppers decoratively around fish. Top with half the tuna sauce and sprinkle with capers. Garnish with lemon slices and parsley sprigs. Offer remaining tuna sauce to add to taste. Makes 8 servings.

Per serving: 562 calories (29% calories from fat), 18 g total fat, 3 g saturated fat, 77 mg cholesterol, 1,201 mg sodium, 60 g carbohydrates, 2 g fiber, 39 g protein, 115 mg calcium, 5 mg iron

Roast Beef with Prunes & Port
(recipe on page 48)

Meats

Red meat is rich-tasting, succulent, satisfying—and a natural for low-fat Italian meals. Just choose well-trimmed cuts of beef, lamb, pork, or veal; then keep the portion sizes modest and the seasonings and accompaniments lean, as we do in Roast Beef with Prunes & Port, Skewered Lamb with Blackberry-Balsamic Glaze, and the other superb dishes in this chapter. Even zesty Italian sausage has a place on lean menus, as Sausage Calzones deliciously prove.

To make this Italian version of all-American roast beef, you baste the meat with a port marinade and serve it with poached prunes.

....

1	beef triangle tip (tri-tip) or top round roast (about 2 lbs./905 g), trimmed of fat
1¾	cups (420 ml) port
⅓	cup (73 g) firmly packed brown sugar
1	can (about 14½ oz./400 g) beef broth
2½	cups (about 1 lb./455 g) pitted prunes
2	packages (about 10 oz./285 g *each*) frozen tiny onions, thawed
1	pound (455 g) dried farfalle (pasta bow ties)
2	cloves garlic, minced
2	tablespoons chopped fresh oregano or 2 teaspoons dried oregano
	Oregano sprigs
	Salt and pepper

....

1. Set beef in a 9- by 13-inch (23- by 33-cm) baking pan. Set aside. In a 3- to 4-quart (2.8- to 3.8-liter) pan, combine port and sugar; stir over medium heat just until sugar is dissolved. Remove from heat and let

Roast Beef with Prunes & Port

....

Preparation time: 20 minutes
Cooking time: About 50 minutes
Pictured on page 46

cool slightly; then measure out ⅓ cup (80 ml) of the port mixture to use for basting and set it aside. Add broth, prunes, and onions to port mixture remaining in pan; set aside.

2. Roast meat in a 450°F (230°C) oven, basting 4 times with the ⅓ cup (80 ml) port mixture, until a meat thermometer inserted in thickest part registers 135°F (57°C) for rare (about 35 minutes). After 25 minutes, check temperature every 5 to 10 minutes. If pan appears dry, add water, 4 to 6 tablespoons (60 to 90 ml) at a time, stirring to scrape browned bits free from pan bottom; do not let drippings scorch.

3. While meat is roasting, bring prune mixture to a boil over high heat. Then reduce heat and boil gently, uncovered, until prunes and onions are very soft (about 30 minutes). Remove from heat; keep warm.

4. When meat is done, transfer to a carving board, cover loosely, and let stand for about 15 minutes. Meanwhile, in a 6- to 8-quart (6- to 8-liter) pan, bring about 4 quarts (3.8 liters) water to a boil over medium-high heat; stir in pasta and cook until just tender to bite, 8 to 10 minutes. (Or cook pasta according to package directions.) Drain pasta well; then transfer to a large rimmed platter, mix in garlic and chopped oregano, and keep warm.

5. Pour any meat drippings from baking pan into prune mixture; also add any meat juices that have accumulated on board. With a slotted spoon, ladle prunes and onions over and around pasta; transfer cooking liquid to a small pitcher.

6. To serve, thinly slice meat across the grain and arrange over pasta mixture. Garnish with oregano sprigs. Offer cooking liquid to pour over meat and pasta and season to taste with salt and pepper. Makes 8 servings.

....

Per serving: 581 calories (8% calories from fat), 5 g total fat, 1 g saturated fat, 65 mg cholesterol, 427 mg sodium, 99 g carbohydrates, 6 g fiber, 36 g protein, 87 mg calcium, 7 mg iron

Plump dried cherries poached in Cabernet accompany this herb-rubbed beef roast.

....

1½ teaspoons *each* whole black peppercorns, dried thyme, and grated orange peel

½ teaspoon *each* dried oregano and coriander seeds

¼ teaspoon ground cinnamon

⅛ teaspoon ground allspice

4 cloves garlic, minced or pressed

1 trimmed, tied center-cut beef tenderloin (about 5 lbs./2.3 kg)

3½ cups (830 ml) beef broth

1¾ cups (420 ml) Cabernet Sauvignon

3 cups (about 15 oz./425 g) dried pitted tart cherries

¼ cup (60 ml) red currant jelly

2 tablespoons cornstarch blended with ¼ cup (60 ml) cold water

6 large oranges (about 3 lbs./ 1.35 kg *total*), thinly sliced

Salt and pepper

....

1. In a small bowl, mix peppercorns, thyme, orange peel, oregano,

Beef Tenderloin with Cabernet-Cherry Sauce

....

Preparation time: 25 minutes
Cooking time: 35 to 50 minutes
Standing time: 15 minutes

coriander seeds, cinnamon, allspice, and garlic. Rub mixture over beef; then set beef in a 10- by 15-inch (25- by 38-cm) roasting pan. Roast in a 450°F (230°C) oven until a meat thermometer inserted in thickest part registers 135°F (57°C) for rare (35 to 40 minutes), 140°F (60°C) for medium (about 50 minutes). Starting about 10 minutes before meat is done, check temperature every 5 to 10 minutes. If pan appears dry, add water, 4 to 6 tablespoons (60 to 90 ml) at a time, stirring to scrape browned bits free from pan bottom; do not let drippings scorch.

2. Meanwhile, in a 3- to 4-quart (2.8- to 3.8-liter) pan, combine

2 cups (470 ml) of the broth, wine, cherries, and jelly; bring to a boil over high heat. Then reduce heat, cover, and simmer until cherries are softened (15 to 20 minutes). Remove from heat.

3. When meat is done, transfer it to a large platter. Snip and discard strings. Cover meat loosely and let stand for about 15 minutes. Meanwhile, add remaining 1½ cups (360 ml) broth to roasting pan; place over medium heat and stir to scrape browned bits free from pan bottom. Pour broth mixture into cherry mixture; bring to a boil, stirring often. Add cornstarch mixture and stir until sauce boils and thickens slightly. Pour into a bowl and keep warm.

4. Garnish meat with orange slices. To serve, slice meat across the grain and offer sauce to spoon over it; season to taste with salt and pepper. Makes about 16 servings.

....

Per serving: 362 calories (30% calories from fat), 11 g total fat, 4 g saturated fat, 88 mg cholesterol, 440 mg sodium, 30 g carbohydrates, 2 g fiber, 30 g protein, 45 mg calcium, 4 mg iron

Each slice of this big special-occasion meat loaf sports a colorful spiral of herb-and-cheese filling.

....

- 1 cup (about 2 oz./55 g) dried tomatoes (not packed in oil)
- 2 tablespoons (30 ml) Marsala
- 1 teaspoon olive oil
- 1 large red onion (about 12 oz./340 g), chopped
- 5 slices sourdough sandwich bread (about 5 oz./140 g *total*), torn into pieces
- 1½ pounds (680 g) lean ground beef
- 4 ounces (115 g) reduced-fat or regular mild Italian sausage, casings removed and meat crumbled
- 1 large jar (about 4 oz./115 g) diced pimentos, drained
- 1 large egg
- 2 large egg whites
- 2 cloves garlic, minced or pressed
- ½ teaspoon dried thyme
- ¼ teaspoon ground sage
- ⅓ cup (20 g) chopped Italian or regular parsley
- ¼ cup (20 g) grated Parmesan cheese
- ¼ teaspoon pepper
- 1⅓ cups (193 g) dried currants
- 1¼ cups (50 g) lightly packed fresh basil leaves
- 1 ounce (28 g) thinly sliced prosciutto, coarsely chopped
- ¼ cup (28 g) shredded fontina cheese
- ¼ cup (35 g) yellow cornmeal
  Italian or regular parsley sprigs

Spiral Stuffed Meat Loaf

....

Preparation time: 35 minutes
Cooking time: About 1½ hours
Pictured on facing page

1. Place tomatoes in a small bowl and add boiling water to cover. Let stand until soft (about 10 minutes), stirring occasionally. Drain well; gently squeeze out excess liquid. Finely chop tomatoes and return to bowl. Drizzle with Marsala and set aside.

2. Heat oil in a wide nonstick frying pan over medium-high heat. Add onion and cook, stirring often, until it begins to brown (about 10 min-

utes); add water, ¼ cup (60 ml) at a time, if pan appears dry. Transfer onion to a large bowl and let cool slightly.

3. In a food processor or blender, whirl bread to form fine crumbs. Add crumbs to onion in bowl. Add beef, sausage, pimentos, egg, egg whites, garlic, thyme, sage, chopped parsley, Parmesan cheese, and pepper; mix until very well blended.

4. On a large sheet of parchment paper or wax paper, pat meat mixture into a 10- by 15-inch (25- by 38-cm) rectangle. Distribute chopped tomatoes, currants, basil leaves, prosciutto, and fontina cheese over meat in even layers to within 1 inch (2.5 cm) of edges. Using paper to help you, lift narrow end of rectangle nearest you over filling; then carefully roll up meat to form a cylinder. Pinch seam and ends closed. Dust a 9- by 13-inch (23- by 33-cm) baking dish with cornmeal; using 2 wide spatulas, transfer loaf to dish.

5. Bake in a 350°F (175°C) oven until loaf is well browned on top (about 1¼ hours); add water, ¼ cup (60 ml) at a time, if dish appears dry. With wide spatulas, carefully transfer loaf to a platter. Serve hot or cold. Garnish with parsley sprigs. Makes 8 to 10 servings.

....

Per serving: 369 calories (30% calories from fat), 13 g total fat, 5 g saturated fat, 82 mg cholesterol, 384 mg sodium, 39 g carbohydrates, 4 g fiber, 27 g protein, 183 mg calcium, 5 mg iron

Spiral Stuffed Meat Loaf
(recipe on facing page)

The Essence of Olive Oil

In this book, our cooking fat of choice is often olive oil—for two reasons. First, this monounsaturated oil is widely used in Italy; second, recent research suggests that it may carry some health benefits, possibly helping to reduce cholesterol levels.

Which olive oil should you use? In the market, you'll find extra-virgin, virgin, pure, even "light" oils. On this page, we tell you how these oils are made—and what characterizes each type.

What Gives Olive Oil Its Flavor?

An olive oil's character and quality are determined by the variety of fruit and by how it is cultivated, harvested, handled (olives are fragile), and pressed.

Olives for oil can be harvested over several months. Mature green fruit picked in early fall yields oil that is typically green in color, with a raw, sharp flavor often described as acrid, beany, bell pepperish, grassy, herbaceous, leafy, or woodsy. Riper fruit, harvested from early winter to early spring, yields proportionally more oil than greener olives. The oil is usually golden; it's fruitier, smoother, and more velvety in flavor and mouth feel than early-harvest oils.

If an olive oil was made exclusively from a specific harvest period, the label may provide that information. But producers often make oil from several harvests through a season, then blend them to yield oils combining the vigor of early-harvest oils with the softness of late-harvest ones.

How Is It Made?

Olives are crushed with their pits to make a thick paste called mash, which is either pressed or centrifuged to separate the oil from the rest of the mash. The oil rises to the top of the mixture and is then skimmed off; if the mash was centrifuged, the oil, too, is centrifuged a second time. Finally, the oil is aged for 3 to 6 months to mellow its natural bitterness.

Grades of Olive Oil

The International Olive Oil Council in Madrid sets the legal definitions for olive oil grades. Oil is evaluated by two subjective measures—smell and taste—and by one objective measure, namely, the level of free oleic acids (the predominant fatty acid in olive oil). Differences in grade are based on the latter measure: the lower the percentage of free oleic acids, the higher the oil quality.

Oils with 1% or less free oleic acids are *extra-virgin*— the top grade. Those with over 1% but no more than 3.3% of these acids are *virgin* olive oils. *Pure* olive oil is a blend with no more than 3.3% acidity. Any oils with over 3.3% free oleic acids are refined using heat, a process that makes them neutral in color, flavor, and aroma. To give such oils more personality, producers blend them with extra-virgin or virgin oil and sell them as "pure olive oil" or, more frequently, as just "olive oil."

You'll also encounter olive oils with "light" on the label. These are refined specifically to make them taste like mild vegetable oils; despite the word "light," they have the same fat and calorie content as any other olive oil.

Because extra-virgin oil delivers the best flavor, it commands the highest price. Be aware, though, that high grades of olive oil don't always live up to their label: due to the fact that there is no regulatory agency to enforce the official definitions, many manufacturers dilute extra-virgin oil with refined oils, yet still label the product "extra-virgin." Your best tactic is to sample different brands until you find an extra-virgin oil with the flavor you want.

Buying & Storing Olive Oil

For the clearest impression of an oil's flavor, dip a chunk of bread into the oil and taste it. For seasoning salads, vegetables, sauces, and breads, any oil with a flavor you like is fine. For cooking, pure or refined olive oil works well; using extra-virgin oil is extravagant, as heat lessens its flavor.

Good-quality olive oil is quite stable compared with polyunsaturated oils. If bottled airtight and stored in a cool, dark place, unopened olive oil stays fresh-tasting for up to 2 years. If refrigerated, it turns cloudy and solidifies; once returned to room temperature, it will clear again, but frequent chilling and warming start a breakdown that leads rapidly to rancidity.

Even after opening, olive oil keeps longer than polyunsaturated oils. Stored in a tightly closed container in a cool, dark place, it should stay fresh for 6 months to a year.

For a quick meal, try these sausage-topped, sautéed veal scallops, served with a lemony mustard sauce made from the pan drippings.

Veal Capocollo

Preparation time: 20 minutes
Cooking time: About 10 minutes

- 6 **very thin slices capocollo (or coppa) sausage (about 1½ oz./43 g *total*)**
- 6 **slices veal scaloppine (about 1 lb./455 g *total*)**
- 1 **teaspoon olive oil**
- 4 **green onions, thinly sliced diagonally**
- 2 **cloves garlic, minced**
- ¼ **cup (60 ml) beef broth**
- 2 **tablespoons (30 ml) Dijon mustard**
- 1 **tablespoon (15 ml) lemon juice**
- 1½ **teaspoons chopped fresh basil or ½ teaspoon dried basil**

  Lemon slices and basil sprigs

1. Lay a slice of sausage on each veal slice, pressing lightly so that meat and sausage stick together. Set aside.

2. Heat oil in a wide nonstick frying pan over medium heat. Add onions and garlic; stir often until onions are soft but still bright green (about 3 minutes). Push onion mixture aside; place veal in pan, overlapping slices as little as possible. Cook, turning once, just until veal is no longer pink in center; cut to test (about 3 minutes). With a slotted spatula, transfer veal slices, sausage side up, to a platter; keep warm.

3. Working quickly, add broth, mustard, lemon juice, and chopped basil to pan; stir to blend. Cook over medium-high heat, stirring, until mixture boils and thickens slightly. Drizzle sauce over meat; garnish with lemon slices and basil sprigs. Makes 4 servings.

Per serving: 172 calories (22% calories from fat), 4 g total fat, 1 g saturated fat, 94 mg cholesterol, 509 mg sodium, 6 g carbohydrates, 0.4 g fiber, 27 g protein, 45 mg calcium, 2 mg iron

---

Marinated in a blend of purple jam, vinegar, and mustard, this lamb cooks quickly on the grill.

Skewered Lamb with Blackberry-Balsamic Glaze

Preparation time: 20 minutes
Marinating time: At least 1 hour
Cooking time: About 8 minutes

- ½ **cup (120 ml) blackberry jam**
- ⅓ **cup (80 ml) balsamic vinegar**
- 1 **tablespoon (15 ml) Dijon mustard**
- 1 **tablespoon chopped fresh rosemary or 1 teaspoon dried rosemary**
- 1½ **pounds (680 g) lean boneless lamb (such as leg or loin), trimmed of fat and cut into 1-inch (2.5-cm) cubes**

  Salt

1. In a large bowl, stir together jam, vinegar, mustard, and rosemary.

Pour a third of the mixture into a small container; cover and refrigerate. Add lamb to remaining jam mixture in bowl. Stir well, cover, and refrigerate for at least 1 hour or until next day.

2. Lift meat cubes from bowl and thread equally on four to six 12- to 14-inch (30- to 35.5-cm) metal skewers; discard marinade left in bowl. Place skewers on a lightly oiled grill 4 to 6 inches (10 to 15 cm) above a solid bed of medium-hot coals. Cook, turning and basting with reserved jam mixture, until meat is evenly browned and done to your liking; cut to test (about 8 minutes for medium-rare).

3. Push meat from skewers onto plates. Season to taste with salt. Makes 4 servings.

Per serving: 324 calories (28% calories from fat), 10 g total fat, 4 g saturated fat, 114 mg cholesterol, 168 mg sodium, 20 g carbohydrates, 0.4 g fiber, 37 g protein, 19 mg calcium, 3 mg iron

Stuffed Lamb Chops with Creamy Polenta
(recipe on facing page)

Tangy blue cheese and toasted pine nuts fill these grilled lamb chops. Serve them with hot polenta studded with corn kernels.

8 small lamb rib chops (*each about 1 inch/2.5 cm thick; about 2 lbs./905 g total*), trimmed of fat

½ small onion, cut into chunks

¼ cup (60 ml) reduced-sodium soy sauce

2 tablespoons firmly packed brown sugar

2 tablespoons (30 ml) lemon juice

1 large clove garlic, peeled

¼ cup (65 g) pine nuts or slivered almonds

¼ cup (62 g) packed crumbled blue-veined cheese

Pepper

2 cups (470 ml) low-fat (1%) milk

½ cup (120 ml) beef broth

1 cup (138 g) polenta or yellow cornmeal

1 large can (about 15 oz./425 g) cream-style corn

1 teaspoon chopped fresh thyme or ¼ teaspoon dried thyme

½ teaspoon salt

1 cup (about 8 oz./230 g) nonfat ricotta cheese

¼ cup (20 g) grated Parmesan cheese

Thyme sprigs

Stuffed Lamb Chops with Creamy Polenta

Preparation time: 30 minutes
Marinating time: At least 30 minutes
Cooking time: About 25 minutes
Pictured on facing page

1. With a sharp knife, cut a horizontal 1½-inch-wide (3.5-cm-wide) pocket in each lamb chop, starting from meaty side and cutting through to bone. Set chops aside.

2. In a food processor or blender, combine onion, soy sauce, sugar, lemon juice, and garlic. Whirl until smoothly puréed. Pour into a heavy-duty resealable plastic food-storage bag. Add chops; seal bag and rotate to coat chops with marinade. Refrigerate for at least 30 minutes or up to 6 hours, turning bag over occasionally.

3. Toast pine nuts in a small frying pan over medium heat until golden (about 3 minutes), stirring often; then pour into a small bowl and let cool slightly. Add blue-veined cheese and mix well. Season to taste with pepper, cover, and refrigerate until ready to use.

4. When you are almost ready to grill chops, prepare polenta. In a 4- to 5-quart (3.8- to 5-liter) pan, bring milk and broth just to a boil over medium-high heat. Stir in polenta, corn, chopped thyme, and salt. Reduce heat and simmer, uncovered, stirring often and scraping pan bottom with a long-handled spoon (mixture will spatter), until polenta tastes creamy (about 15 minutes). Stir in ricotta cheese; then remove pan from heat, stir in Parmesan cheese, and keep warm.

5. Lift chops from bag; drain, reserving marinade. Using a spoon, stuff an eighth of the cheese–pine nut filling deep into pocket of each chop. Place chops on a greased grill 4 to 6 inches (10 to 15 cm) above a solid bed of hot coals. Cook, basting twice with marinade and turning once, until chops are evenly browned and done to your liking; cut in thickest part to test (6 to 8 minutes for medium-rare).

6. To serve, divide polenta among 4 individual plates; arrange 2 chops on each plate alongside polenta. Garnish with thyme sprigs. Makes 4 servings.

Per serving: 660 calories (30% calories from fat), 22 g total fat, 8 g saturated fat, 94 mg cholesterol, 1,823 mg sodium, 68 g carbohydrates, 4 g fiber, 48 g protein, 604 mg calcium, 5 mg iron

Originating in Naples, calzone is reminiscent of a stuffed pizza. These individual calzones have a zesty sausage and cheese filling.

- 1 package active dry yeast
- 1 cup (240 ml) warm water (about 110°F/43°C)
  About 2½ cups (310 g) all-purpose flour
  About ½ cup (70 g) yellow cornmeal
- 1 tablespoon sugar
- ½ teaspoon salt
- 3 tablespoons (45 ml) olive oil
- 1 pound (455 g) reduced-fat or regular mild Italian sausage, casings removed and meat crumbled
- 1 large onion, chopped
- ¼ teaspoon *each* dried marjoram, dried rubbed sage, and dried thyme
- 1 large tomato (about 8 oz./230 g), chopped
- 1 carton (about 15 oz./425 g) nonfat ricotta cheese
- ½ cup (50 g) fine dry bread crumbs
- ⅓ cup (30 g) grated Romano cheese
- ⅓ cup (20 g) chopped Italian or regular parsley
- 2 tablespoons drained capers (or to taste)

Sausage Calzones

Preparation time: 35 minutes
Rising time: 45 to 60 minutes
Cooking time: 25 to 30 minutes

1. In a small bowl, sprinkle yeast over warm water; let stand until foamy (about 5 minutes). In a large bowl, mix 2½ cups (310 g) of the flour, ½ cup (70 g) of the cornmeal, sugar, and salt. Add yeast mixture and 2 tablespoons (30 ml) of the oil. Stir until dough is evenly moistened. *To knead by hand,* scrape dough onto a lightly floured board and knead until smooth and springy (about 10 minutes), adding more flour as needed to prevent sticking. *To knead with a dough hook,* beat dough on medium speed until it pulls cleanly from sides of bowl and is springy (5 to 7 minutes); if dough is sticky, add more flour, 1 tablespoon at a time.

2. Place dough in a greased bowl; turn over to grease top. Cover bowl with plastic wrap; let dough rise in a warm, draft-free place until almost doubled (45 to 60 minutes). Or let rise in refrigerator until next day.

3. Meanwhile, in a wide nonstick frying pan, combine sausage, onion, marjoram, sage, and thyme. Cook over medium-high heat, stirring often, until meat is tinged with brown (10 to 15 minutes); add water, 1 tablespoon (15 ml) at a time, if pan appears dry. Transfer mixture to a large bowl; let cool slightly. Stir in tomato, ricotta cheese, bread crumbs, Romano cheese, parsley, and capers; set aside.

4. Punch dough down, turn out onto a lightly floured board, and knead briefly to release air. Divide dough into 6 equal balls; roll each ball into an 8-inch (20-cm) round. Spoon a sixth of the sausage filling over half of each dough round, spreading it to within ½ inch (1 cm) of edge; fold plain half of round over filling and pinch edges firmly to seal.

5. Dust 2 greased large baking sheets with cornmeal. With a wide spatula, transfer calzones to baking sheets. Prick tops of calzones with a fork; brush lightly with remaining 1 tablespoon (15 ml) oil.

6. Bake in a 425°F (220°C) oven until richly browned (about 15 minutes), switching positions of baking sheets halfway through baking. Let cool for at least 5 minutes before serving; serve hot or warm. Makes 6 servings.

Per serving: 595 calories (30% calories from fat), 20 g total fat, 5 g saturated fat, 26 mg cholesterol, 1,062 mg sodium, 70 g carbohydrates, 4 g fiber, 33 g protein, 472 mg calcium, 5 mg iron

Served over pasta ribbons and topped with cheese, this sturdy three-meat stew is delightful for supper on a chilly day.

....

1 tablespoon (15 ml) olive oil

1 pound (455 g) *each* boneless pork, beef, and veal stew meat, trimmed of fat and cut into ½-inch (1-cm) cubes

1 large onion, chopped

1 large carrot (about 4 oz./115 g), chopped

8 ounces (230 g) mushrooms, thinly sliced

1 cup (120 g) thinly sliced celery

1 large can (about 28 oz./795 g) tomatoes

1 can (about 15 oz./425 g) tomato purée

½ cup (120 ml) dry red wine

1 tablespoon chopped fresh rosemary or 1 teaspoon dried rosemary

⅛ to ¼ teaspoon fennel seeds

2 pounds (905 g) dried fettuccine

1 cup (about 3 oz./85 g) grated Parmesan cheese

Salt and crushed red pepper flakes

Pork, Beef & Veal Ragout with Fettuccine

....

Preparation time: 30 minutes
Cooking time: About 1½ hours

1. Heat oil in a 4- to 5-quart (3.8- to 5-liter) pan over medium-high heat. Add pork, beef, and veal, a portion at a time (do not crowd pan). Cook, stirring often, until meat is tinged with brown (about 5 minutes). As meat is browned, use a slotted spoon to transfer it to a large bowl; set aside.

2. Add onion, carrot, mushrooms, celery, and 1 tablespoon (15 ml) water to pan. Cook, stirring often, just until vegetables are soft (about 15 minutes). Return meat (and any juices that have accumulated in bowl) to pan; then add tomatoes (break up with a spoon) and their liquid, tomato purée, wine, rosemary, and fennel seeds. Bring to a boil over high heat, stirring often. Then reduce heat, cover, and sim-

mer until meat is tender when pierced (about 1 hour); stir occasionally at first, then more often near end of cooking time, watching closely to prevent scorching.

3. About 20 minutes before stew is done, bring about 6 quarts (6 liters) water to a boil in an 8- to 10-quart (8- to 10-liter) pan over medium-high heat; stir in pasta and cook until just tender to bite, 8 to 10 minutes. (Or cook pasta according to package directions.) Drain pasta well and divide among wide individual bowls; top with stew. Sprinkle with cheese. Season to taste with salt and red pepper flakes. Makes 10 servings.

....

Per serving: 638 calories (23% calories from fat), 16 g total fat, 5 g saturated fat, 192 mg cholesterol, 594 mg sodium, 77 g carbohydrates, 5 g fiber, 45 g protein, 198 mg calcium, 8 mg iron

Start by browning veal shanks in a very hot oven, then cover and bake. When the meat is tender enough to pull apart, make risotto the easy way: stir rice into the pan juices and continue to bake, letting the grains absorb the flavorful liquid.

- 2 tablespoons (30 ml) olive oil
- 5 to 6 pounds (2.3 to 2.7 kg) meaty veal shanks (*each about 2 inches/5 cm thick*)
- 1 cup (240 ml) dry red wine
- 4 cups (950 ml) beef broth
- 2 tablespoons grated lemon peel
- 1 teaspoon *each* dried thyme and dried basil
- 2 cups (390 g) medium- or short-grain white rice
- 1 cup (130 g) chopped carrots
- ¼ cup (15 g) chopped Italian or regular parsley
- 2 cloves garlic, minced or pressed
- 1 cup (130 g) chopped zucchini
- 1 cup (150 g) chopped red bell pepper
- ½ cup (40 g) grated Parmesan cheese
- Lemon wedges
- Italian or regular parsley sprigs

Osso Buco with Risotto

Preparation time: 20 minutes
Cooking time: About 2½ hours
Pictured on facing page

1. Place oil in an 11- by 17-inch (28- by 43-cm) roasting pan. Heat in a 475°F (245°C) oven until hot (about 1 minute). Lay veal shanks in pan in a single layer. Bake, uncovered, for 30 minutes; then turn meat over and continue to bake until browned (about 10 more minutes).

2. Remove pan from oven and add wine; stir to scrape browned bits free from pan bottom. Then stir in broth, 1 tablespoon of the lemon peel, thyme, and basil; stir again, scraping browned bits free. Cover pan tightly with foil and bake until meat is tender enough to pull apart easily (about 1½ hours).

3. Uncover pan; stir 2½ cups (590 ml) water, rice, and carrots into pan juices. Bake, uncovered, stirring rice and turning meat over occasionally, until liquid has been absorbed and rice is tender to bite (20 to 25 minutes). If rice begins to dry out, add more water, about ½ cup (120 ml) at a time.

4. In a small bowl, mix remaining 1 tablespoon lemon peel, chopped parsley, and garlic. Remove meat from pan, transfer to a large platter, and sprinkle with parsley mixture. Stir zucchini and bell pepper into rice mixture; spoon rice mixture onto platter alongside meat, then sprinkle with cheese. Garnish with lemon wedges and parsley sprigs. Makes 4 to 6 servings.

Per serving: 581 calories (18% calories from fat), 11 g total fat, 3 g saturated fat, 134 mg cholesterol, 770 mg sodium, 69 g carbohydrates, 2 g fiber, 47 g protein, 155 mg calcium, 6 mg iron

Osso Buco with Risotto
(recipe on facing page)

Focaccia

Grape-studded Focaccia

Preparation time: 25 minutes
Rising time: 1½ to 2 hours
Cooking time: 30 to 35 minutes

·······················

Focaccia Dough
(recipe follows); or
2 loaves (about 1 lb./
455 g *each*) frozen
white bread dough,
thawed and kneaded
together

1   tablespoon (15 ml)
olive oil

40 to 50 seedless red
grapes (6 to 8 oz./
170 to 230 g *total*)

1   tablespoon chopped
fresh rosemary or
1 teaspoon dried
rosemary

Coarse salt and
coarsely ground
pepper

3   ounces (85 g)
pancetta or bacon,
coarsely chopped

·······················

1. Prepare Focaccia
Dough. When dough is
almost doubled, punch it
down, turn out onto a
lightly floured board, and
knead briefly to release
air. Roll dough into a 9-
by 12-inch (23- by 30-cm)
rectangle about ½ inch (1
cm) thick. Fold rectangle
loosely in half; transfer to
an oiled shallow 10- by
15-inch (25- by 38-cm)
baking pan and unfold.

Press and stretch dough
to cover pan evenly. If
dough is too elastic, let it
rest for about 5 minutes,
then press again. Cover
dough lightly with plastic
wrap and let rise in a
warm, draft-free place
until almost doubled
(45 to 60 minutes).

2. Brush oil lightly over
dough. With your finger-
tips, gently press dough
down all over, giving surface a dimpled look. Also
press dough gently into
corners of pan. Press
grapes in even rows into
dimpled dough, spacing
them about 1 inch (2.5 cm)
apart. Sprinkle with rosemary, then with salt and
pepper.

3. Bake in a 400°F (205°C)
oven until focaccia is well
browned at edges and on
bottom (30 to 35 min-
utes); after 20 minutes,
sprinkle with pancetta.
If topping is browned
before bread is done,
cover loosely with foil.
Serve hot or warm.
Makes 12 servings.

Focaccia Dough. In a
large bowl, sprinkle 1
package **active dry yeast**
over 1½ cups (360 ml)
warm water (about
110°F/43°C); let stand
until foamy (about 5 min-
utes). Stir in ½ teaspoon
salt and 2 tablespoons

(30 ml) **olive oil.** Add 2½
cups (310 g) **all-purpose
flour;** stir to blend. Beat
with an electric mixer on
high speed until dough is
glossy and stretchy (3 to
5 minutes). Stir in 1⅓ cups
(165 g) more **all-purpose
flour.**

To knead by hand, scrape
dough onto a lightly
floured board and knead
until smooth and springy
(about 10 minutes), adding
more flour as needed to
prevent sticking.

*To knead with a dough
hook,* beat dough on medium speed until it pulls
cleanly from sides of
bowl and is springy (5 to
7 minutes); if dough is
sticky, add more flour,
1 tablespoon at a time.

Place dough in a
greased bowl and turn
over to grease top. Cover
bowl with plastic wrap;
let dough rise in a warm,
draft-free place until
almost doubled (45 to 60
minutes). Or let rise in
refrigerator until next day.

Per serving: 214 calories
(27% calories from fat), 6 g total
fat, 1 g saturated fat, 4 mg cholesterol, 167 mg sodium, 33 g
carbohydrates, 1 g fiber, 5 g protein, 10 mg calcium, 2 mg iron

Pear & Pepper Focaccia

Preparation time: 25 minutes
Rising time: 45 to 60 minutes
Cooking time: About 30 minutes

·······················

1   loaf (about 1 lb./455 g)
frozen white bread
dough, thawed

3   tablespoons (45 ml)
lemon juice

3   medium-size firm-
ripe pears (about
18 oz./510 g *total*)

1½ cups (90 g) firmly
packed Italian or
regular parsley sprigs

3   tablespoons (45 ml)
olive oil

1   tablespoon grated
lemon peel

2   tablespoons sugar

½   to 1 teaspoon coarse-
ly ground pepper

⅓   cup (30 g) grated
Parmesan cheese

·······················

1. Place dough in a non-
stick or lightly oiled shallow 10- by 15-inch (25- by
38-cm) baking pan; press
and push to cover pan
evenly. If dough is too
elastic, let it rest for a few
minutes, then press again.
Cover dough lightly with
plastic wrap and let rise

in a warm, draft-free place until almost doubled (45 to 60 minutes).

2. Meanwhile, pour lemon juice into a medium-size bowl. Core pears and thinly slice into bowl, turning fruit to coat with juice. Also make parsley pesto: in a blender or food processor, combine parsley sprigs, oil, and lemon peel. Whirl until smoothly puréed, scraping sides of container as needed.

3. With your fingertips, gently press dough down all over, giving surface a dimpled look; also press dough gently into corners of pan. Spread pesto evenly over dough. Arrange pear slices on dough and press in gently. Mix sugar and pepper and sprinkle over pears.

4. Bake in a 400°F (205°C) oven until focaccia is well browned at edges and on bottom (about 30 minutes); after 20 minutes, sprinkle with cheese. If topping is browned before bread is done, cover loosely with foil. Serve hot or warm. Makes 12 servings.

Per serving: 176 calories (30% calories from fat), 6 g total fat, 1 g saturated fat, 4 mg cholesterol, 227 mg sodium, 27 g carbohydrates, 1 g fiber, 4 g protein, 58 mg calcium, 1 mg iron

Eggplant & Onion Focaccia

Preparation time: 30 minutes
Rising time: 1½ to 2 hours
Cooking time: 55 to 60 minutes

Focaccia Dough (recipe on facing page); or 2 loaves (about 1 lb./455 g *each*) frozen white bread dough, thawed and kneaded together

2 medium-size eggplants (about 2 lbs./905 g *total*), unpeeled, cut into ¾-inch (2-cm) cubes

1 small red onion (about 8 oz./230 g), cut into ¾-inch (2-cm) cubes

2 tablespoons (30 ml) olive oil

1½ cups (about 6 oz./170 g) shredded smoked or plain part-skim mozzarella cheese (or use smoked Gouda cheese)

2 tablespoons chopped Italian or regular parsley

1. Prepare Focaccia Dough. When dough is almost doubled, punch it down, turn out onto a lightly floured board, and knead briefly to release air. Roll dough into a 9- by 12-inch (23- by 30-cm) rectangle about

½ inch (1 cm) thick. Fold rectangle loosely in half; transfer to an oiled shallow 10- by 15-inch (25- by 38-cm) baking pan and unfold. Press and stretch dough to cover pan evenly. If dough is too elastic, let it rest for about 5 minutes, then press again. Cover dough lightly with plastic wrap and let rise in a warm, draft-free place until almost doubled (45 to 60 minutes).

2. Meanwhile, place eggplant and onion in a large, shallow baking pan. Drizzle with 1 tablespoon (15 ml) of the oil and mix gently; then spread vegetables out evenly. Bake in a 450°F (230°C) oven, stirring occasionally, until eggplant is lightly browned and beginning to soften (about 25 minutes); add water, ¼ cup (60 ml) at a time, if pan appears dry. Remove vegetables from pan and set aside.

3. Brush remaining 1 tablespoon (15 ml) oil lightly over dough. With your fingertips, gently press dough down all over, giving surface a dimpled look. Also press dough gently into corners of pan. Evenly sprinkle cheese over dimpled dough; distribute eggplant mixture over cheese.

4. Bake in a 400°F (205°C) oven until focaccia is well browned at edges and on bottom (30 to 35 minutes). If topping is browned before bread is done, cover loosely with foil. Sprinkle with parsley. Serve hot or warm. Makes 12 servings.

Per serving: 266 calories (30% calories from fat), 9 g total fat, 3 g saturated fat, 20 mg cholesterol, 261 mg sodium, 38 g carbohydrates, 3 g fiber, 9 g protein, 114 mg calcium, 3 mg iron

Portabella Mushroom Sandwiches
(recipe on page 64)

Meatless Main Dishes

For meatless Italian-style meals that are low in fat and naturally great tasting, focus on popular pasta, grains, and legumes. Choices such as Polenta Pepper Torte, Linguine with Lentils, and Orecchiette with Broccoli Rabe & Pine Nuts provide great nutrition and delicious dining, too. And don't forget egg- or cheese-based dishes such as frittata and ricotta pancakes. With a few adjustments, these too can become low-fat favorites.

•

Big portabella mushrooms pan-fried in a cornmeal batter make wholesome, hearty sandwiches. Serve them in crusty rolls spread with chard-and-herb cream cheese; offer Pickled Vegetables (recipe on page 12) alongside.

- 4 **crusty rolls (about 4 oz./115 g each), split into halves**
- 1 **package (about 10 oz./285 g) frozen chopped Swiss chard, thawed and squeezed dry**
- 1 **large package (about 8 oz./230 g) nonfat cream cheese, at room temperature**
- ¾ **cup (85 g) shredded smoked mozzarella or smoked Gouda cheese**
- 2 **tablespoons (30 ml) nonfat mayonnaise**
- 1 **teaspoon Dijon mustard**
- ½ **teaspoon dried rubbed sage**
  About ¼ cup (60 ml) balsamic vinegar
  Pepper
- 3 **large egg whites**
- ¾ **cup (104 g) yellow cornmeal**
- ⅓ **cup (40 g) all-purpose flour**
- ¼ **teaspoon salt**
- 4 **large portabella mushrooms (about 3 oz./85 g each), stems removed**
- 2 **tablespoons (30 ml) olive oil**
- 4 **to 8 green or red leaf lettuce leaves**
- 4 **to 8 large tomato slices**

Portabella Mushroom Sandwiches

Preparation time: 25 minutes
Cooking time: About 20 minutes
Pictured on page 62

1. If needed, pull bread from base and top of each roll to make a shell about ¼ inch (6 mm) thick; reserve bread scraps for other uses, if desired. Arrange roll halves, cut side up, in a broiler pan; broil about 6 inches below heat until lightly toasted (1½ to 2 minutes). Set aside.

2. In a food processor or blender, combine chard, cream cheese, mozzarella cheese, mayonnaise, mustard, and sage. Whirl until chard is finely chopped, scraping sides of container as needed. Brush cut side of roll bottoms lightly with vinegar and sprinkle with pepper. Set aside about a fourth of the chard mixture; divide remaining mixture equally among roll bottoms (you need about ⅓ cup/80 ml per roll). With a spatula, spread chard mixture to fill hollows in rolls evenly.

3. In a wide, shallow bowl, beat egg whites and 2 tablespoons (30 ml) water to blend. In another wide, shallow bowl, stir together cornmeal, flour, and salt. Dip mushrooms in egg white mixture; drain briefly, then dip in cornmeal mixture and press to coat well all over.

4. Heat 1 tablespoon (15 ml) of the oil in a wide nonstick frying pan over medium-high heat. Add 2 of the mushrooms; cook, turning once, until mushrooms are golden on both sides and tender when pierced (5 to 7 minutes). Remove from pan and keep warm. Repeat to cook remaining 2 mushrooms, using remaining 1 tablespoon (15 ml) oil.

5. Working quickly, place 1 or 2 lettuce leaves on each roll bottom; then top each with one hot mushroom and 1 or 2 tomato slices. Spoon reserved chard mixture over tomato slices. Brush cut side of roll tops lightly with vinegar and sprinkle with pepper; close sandwiches and serve immediately. Makes 4 servings.

Per serving: 709 calories (24% calories from fat), 19 g total fat, 5 g saturated fat, 36 mg cholesterol, 1,553 mg sodium, 101 g carbohydrates, 5 g fiber, 33 g protein, 436 mg calcium, 8 mg iron

Because it isn't layered like the traditional dish, this lasagne goes together quickly.

....

- 12 ounces (340 g) dried lasagne
- 2½ cups (590 ml) low-fat (2%) milk
- ¼ cup (32 g) cornstarch
- 1½ teaspoons dried basil
- ½ teaspoon *each* dried rosemary and salt
- ¼ teaspoon ground nutmeg
- 1 cup (about 8 oz./230 g) nonfat ricotta cheese
- 2 packages (about 10 oz./285 g *each*) frozen chopped Swiss chard, thawed and squeezed dry
- 2 large ripe tomatoes (about 1 lb./455 g *total*), chopped
- 2 cups (about 8 oz./230 g) shredded mozzarella cheese

Three-cheese Lasagne with Chard

....

Preparation time: 20 minutes
Cooking time: About 1 hour

....

- ⅓ cup (30 g) grated Parmesan cheese

....

1. In a 5- to 6-quart (5- to 6-liter) pan, bring about 3 quarts (2.8 liters) water to a boil over medium-high heat; stir in pasta and cook until just barely tender to bite, about 8 minutes. Drain pasta well and lay out flat; cover lightly.

2. In pasta-cooking pan, smoothly blend milk, cornstarch, basil, rosemary, salt, and nutmeg. Stir over medium-high heat until mixture boils and thickens slightly (about 5 minutes). Stir in ricotta cheese, chard, tomatoes, and half the mozzarella cheese. Gently stir in pasta.

3. Transfer mixture to a 9- by 13-inch (23- by 33-cm) baking pan; gently push pasta down to cover it with sauce. Sprinkle with remaining mozzarella cheese, then with Parmesan cheese. Bake in a 375°F (190°C) oven until lasagne is bubbly in center (about 40 minutes). Let stand for about 5 minutes before serving. Makes 8 servings.

....

Per serving: 362 calories (24% calories from fat), 10 g total fat, 5 g saturated fat, 33 mg cholesterol, 531 mg sodium, 48 g carbohydrates, 3 g fiber, 22 g protein, 499 mg calcium, 3 mg iron

---

Creamy cannellini beans are the base of this easy vegetable stew.

....

- 6 slices Italian sandwich bread (about 6 oz./ 170 g *total*), cut into ½-inch (1-cm) cubes
- 2 teaspoons olive oil
- 2 large onions, chopped
- 4 cloves garlic, minced
- ½ teaspoon *each* dried rubbed sage, dried thyme, and dried marjoram
- ¼ cup (10 g) chopped fresh basil
- 4 large tomatoes (about 2 lbs./ 905 g *total*), chopped
- 3 cans (about 15 oz./425 g *each*) cannellini (white kidney beans), drained and rinsed
- 1 cup (240 ml) canned vegetable broth
- 1 tablespoon (15 ml) red wine vinegar

Tuscan Bean Stew

....

Preparation time: 25 minutes
Cooking time: About 45 minutes

....

- ¼ cup (20 g) grated Parmesan cheese

....

1. Toast bread cubes as directed for Garbanzo Beans with Olive Pesto (page 26). Set aside.

2. Heat oil in a 4- to 5-quart (3.8- to 5-liter) pan over medium-high heat. Add onions, garlic, sage, thyme, marjoram, and ¼ cup (60 ml) water. Cook, stirring often, until onions are soft (about 5 minutes). Add water, 1 tablespoon (15 ml) at a time,

if pan appears dry. Stir in basil and half the tomatoes. Cook, stirring often, just until tomatoes are soft (about 3 minutes). Remove from heat and let cool slightly.

3. Transfer onion mixture to a food processor or blender; whirl until smoothly puréed. Return purée to pan and add beans, broth, and vinegar. Bring to a boil over medium-high heat; then reduce heat, cover, and simmer for 15 minutes.

4. Stir croutons into bean stew; spoon stew into individual bowls. Sprinkle remaining tomatoes around edge of each bowl. Sprinkle with cheese and serve at once. Makes 4 servings.

....

Per serving: 505 calories (12% calories from fat), 7 g total fat, 2 g saturated fat, 4 mg cholesterol, 1,716 mg sodium, 89 g carbohydrates, 25 g fiber, 25 g protein, 260 mg calcium, 7 mg iron

Sure to become a family favorite, this layered eggplant-tomato casserole is a satisfying choice for casual company meals as well.

....

3 large egg whites

3 tablespoons (45 ml) Marsala

1 cup (100 g) fine dry bread crumbs

½ cup (40 g) shredded Parmesan cheese

1 tablespoon chopped fresh thyme or ½ teaspoon dried thyme

½ teaspoon salt

2 medium-size eggplants (about 2 lbs./905 g *total*)

¼ cup (35 g) yellow cornmeal

¾ cup (180 ml) nonfat sour cream

2 cloves garlic, peeled

2 teaspoons cornstarch

1 teaspoon honey

3 cans (about 14½ oz./410 g *each*) diced tomatoes, drained well

1 tablespoon chopped fresh basil or ½ teaspoon dried basil

2 large tomatoes (about 1 lb./ 455 g *total*), very thinly sliced

1 cup (about 4 oz./115 g) shredded mozzarella cheese

Thyme sprigs

Eggplant Parmesan

....

Preparation time: 30 minutes
Cooking time: About 1 hour
Pictured on facing page

1. In a wide, shallow bowl, beat egg whites and Marsala to blend. In another wide, shallow bowl, combine bread crumbs, ¼ cup (20 g) of the Parmesan cheese, chopped thyme, and salt; set aside.

2. Cut unpeeled eggplants crosswise into slices about ¼ inch (6 mm) thick. Dip slices in egg white mixture; drain briefly, then dip in crumb mixture and press to coat lightly all over. Arrange eggplant slices on 2 or 3 greased large baking sheets; pat any remaining crumb mixture on slices.

3. Bake in a 400°F (205°C) oven, turning once, until golden brown on both sides (about 30 minutes); switch positions of baking sheets halfway through baking. If any slices begin to brown excessively, remove them and set aside.

4. Meanwhile, sprinkle cornmeal over bottom of a greased 9- by 13-inch (23- by 33-cm) baking pan; set aside. In a food processor or blender, whirl sour cream, garlic, cornstarch, honey, and two-thirds of the canned tomatoes until smoothly puréed. Stir in remaining canned tomatoes and basil.

5. Spoon a third of the tomato sauce over cornmeal in pan; top evenly with a third of the tomato slices. Arrange half the eggplant slices over tomatoes; sprinkle with half the mozzarella cheese. Top evenly with half each of the remaining tomato sauce and tomato slices, then with remaining eggplant. Top with remaining tomato sauce, tomato slices, and mozzarella cheese. Sprinkle with remaining ¼ cup (20 g) Parmesan cheese.

6. Cover and bake in a 400°F (205°C) oven for 15 minutes. Then uncover and continue to bake until sauce is bubbly and casserole is golden on top and hot in center (15 to 20 more minutes). Garnish with thyme sprigs. Makes 6 servings.

....

Per serving: 337 calories (27% calories from fat), 10 g total fat, 4 g saturated fat, 20 mg cholesterol, 938 mg sodium, 44 g carbohydrates, 6 g fiber, 17 g protein, 390 mg calcium, 4 mg iron

Eggplant Parmesan
(recipe on facing page)

Pesto

Originating in Genoa, pesto is an uncooked sauce featuring a variety of crushed or chopped ingredients. On this page, you'll find several versions, including the familiar basil pesto as well as a few more innovative choices.

Though pesto tends to derive over 30% of its calories from fat, it still fits into lean menus. Just use it sparingly, in combination with low-fat ingredients such as pasta, cooked vegetables, or even warm breadsticks.

If you make pesto in advance, cover and chill it, then use within 4 hours. After that, it may darken and (if made with garlic) taste too strongly garlicky.

Basil Pesto

Preparation time: 10 minutes

- **2 cups (80 g) lightly packed fresh basil leaves**
- **½ cup (40 g) grated Parmesan cheese**
- **⅓ cup (80 ml) olive oil**
- **¼ cup (31 g) walnut pieces**
- **2 cloves garlic, peeled**

1. In a food processor or blender, whirl basil, cheese, oil, walnuts, and garlic until smoothly puréed. Makes about 1 cup (240 ml).

Per tablespoon: 69 calories (80% calories from fat), 6 g total fat, 1 g saturated fat, 2 mg cholesterol, 48 mg sodium, 2 g carbohydrates, 0.1 g fiber, 2 g protein, 84 mg calcium, 1 mg iron

Mixed Herb Pesto

Preparation time: 15 minutes

- **2 cups (80 g) lightly packed fresh basil leaves**
- **½ cup (50 g) thinly sliced green onions**
- **⅓ cup (15 g) lightly packed fresh oregano leaves**
- **¼ cup (20 g) grated Parmesan cheese**
- **¼ cup (60 ml) red wine vinegar**
- **2 tablespoons fresh rosemary leaves**
- **2 tablespoons (30 ml) olive oil**
- **¼ to ½ teaspoon pepper**

1. In a food processor or blender, whirl basil, onions, oregano, cheese, vinegar, rosemary, oil, and pepper until smoothly puréed. Makes about 1 cup (240 ml).

Per tablespoon: 29 calories (62% calories from fat), 2 g total fat, 0.5 g saturated fat, 1 mg cholesterol, 25 mg sodium, 2 g carbohydrates, 0.1 g fiber, 0.9 g protein, 74 mg calcium, 1 mg iron

Mint Pesto

Preparation time: 10 minutes
Cooking time: About 3 minutes

- **½ cup (65 g) pine nuts**
- **1 cup (40 g) lightly packed fresh mint leaves**
- **3 cloves garlic, peeled**
- **3 tablespoons (45 ml) olive oil**
- **¼ cup (20 g) grated Parmesan cheese**

1. Stir pine nuts in a wide frying pan over medium heat until golden (about 3 minutes). Pour into a food processor or blender; let cool slightly.

2. To pine nuts, add mint, garlic, oil, and cheese. Whirl until smoothly puréed. Makes about ¾ cup (180 ml).

Per tablespoon: 71 calories (81% calories from fat), 7 g total fat, 1 g saturated fat, 1 mg cholesterol, 31 mg sodium, 1 g carbohydrates, 0.7 g fiber, 2 g protein, 29 mg calcium, 0.8 mg iron

Red Pepper Pesto

Preparation time: 10 minutes

- **1 jar (12 oz./340 g) roasted red peppers, drained, patted dry**
- **1 cup (40 g) lightly packed fresh basil leaves**
- **1 clove garlic, peeled**
- **⅓ cup (30 g) grated Parmesan cheese**
- **Salt and pepper**

1. In a food processor or blender, whirl peppers, basil, garlic, and cheese until basil is finely chopped. Season to taste with salt and pepper. Makes about 1½ cups (360 ml).

Per tablespoon: 14 calories (25% calories from fat), 0.4 g total fat, 0.2 g saturated fat, 0.9 mg cholesterol, 51 mg sodium, 2 g carbohydrates, 0 g fiber, 0.7 g protein, 47 mg calcium, 0.8 mg iron

Pistachio Pesto

Preparation time: 15 minutes

- **¼ cup (30 g) shelled salted roasted pistachio nuts**
- **1 cup (60 g) firmly packed Italian or regular parsley sprigs**
- **¼ cup (60 ml) white wine vinegar**
- **¼ cup (60 ml) canned vegetable broth**
- **2 tablespoons (30 ml) olive oil**

1. In a food processor or blender, whirl pistachios, parsley, vinegar, broth, and oil until smoothly puréed. Makes about ¾ cup (180 ml).

Per tablespoon: 40 calories (77% calories from fat), 4 g total fat, 0.5 g saturated fat, 0 mg cholesterol, 36 mg sodium, 2 g carbohydrates, 0.4 g fiber, 0.8 g protein, 17 mg calcium, 0.8 mg iron

This tempting casserole will remind you of a savory bread pudding. While it bakes, prepare a sweet-tart relish of dried figs, dried cranberries, and fresh pears to serve alongside.

Spinach Torta with Fig Relish

Preparation time: 30 minutes
Cooking time: About 1½ hours

- 1 package (about 10 oz./285 g) frozen chopped spinach, thawed and squeezed dry
- 3 large eggs
- 4 large egg whites
- 2 tablespoons cornstarch
- 2 cloves garlic, peeled
- 1½ teaspoons *each* chopped fresh oregano, fresh marjoram, and fresh sage; or ½ teaspoon *each* dried oregano, dried marjoram, and dried rubbed sage
- 2 cups (470 ml) half-and-half
- 8 slices egg or whole wheat sandwich bread (about 8 oz./230 g *total*), torn into large pieces
- ¾ cup (85 g) shredded fontina or mozzarella cheese
- 1 large firm-ripe pear such as Anjou or Bartlett (about 8 oz./230 g), peeled, cored, and finely chopped
- ⅓ cup (73 g) firmly packed brown sugar
- ⅓ cup (80 ml) red wine vinegar
- 1½ cups dried figs (about 8 oz./230 g), stems removed and fruit quartered
- ¾ cup (68 g) dried cranberries or raisins
- ¾ cup (180 ml) canned vegetable broth
- ⅛ teaspoon *each* pepper, ground cinnamon, and ground nutmeg
- 2 teaspoons Marsala (or to taste)
- ¼ cup (25 g) thinly sliced green onions

1. In a food processor or blender, combine spinach, eggs, egg whites, cornstarch, garlic, oregano, marjoram, and sage. Whirl until smoothly puréed. Transfer to a large bowl and whisk in half-and-half. Add bread and cheese; mix gently but thoroughly. Let stand until bread is softened (about 5 minutes), stirring occasionally.

2. Transfer mixture to an 8-inch-square (20-cm-square) nonstick or greased regular baking pan. Set pan in a larger baking pan; then set on center rack of a 325°F (165°C) oven. Pour boiling water into larger pan up to level of spinach mixture. Bake until top of torta is golden brown and center no longer jiggles when pan is gently shaken (about 1 hour and 35 minutes).

3. Meanwhile, in a wide nonstick frying pan, mix pear, sugar, and vinegar. Add figs, cranberries, broth, pepper, cinnamon, and nutmeg. Bring to a boil over medium-high heat. Then cook, uncovered, stirring often, until almost all liquid has evaporated (about 20 minutes); as mixture thickens, watch carefully and stir more often to prevent scorching. Remove pan from heat and stir in Marsala and onions.

4. To serve, spoon torta from pan; offer fig relish alongside. Makes 6 servings.

Per serving: 549 calories (30% calories from fat), 19 g total fat, 10 g saturated fat, 172 mg cholesterol, 570 mg sodium, 79 g carbohydrates, 6 g fiber, 18 g protein, 338 mg calcium, 4 mg iron

Fettuccine Alfredo
(recipe on facing page)

Alfredo aficionados will enjoy this variation on an Italian classic. Artichoke hearts enhance the tender pasta and its creamy two-cheese sauce.

....

- 2 cans (about 14 oz./400 g *each*) artichoke hearts packed in water, drained and quartered
- 3 tablespoons chopped Italian or regular parsley
- 3 tablespoons thinly sliced green onions
- 12 ounces (340 g) dried fettuccine
- 1 tablespoon butter or olive oil
- 3 cloves garlic, minced
- 1 tablespoon all-purpose flour
- 1½ cups (360 ml) low-fat (2%) milk
- 1 large package (about 8 oz./ 230 g) nonfat cream cheese, cut into small chunks
- 1½ cups (about 4½ oz./130 g) shredded Parmesan cheese
- ⅛ teaspoon ground nutmeg (optional)
  Pepper

Fettuccine Alfredo

....
Preparation time: 15 minutes
Cooking time: About 25 minutes
Pictured on facing page

1. In a medium-size bowl, combine artichokes, parsley, and onions. Set aside.

2. In a 5- to 6-quart (5- to 6-liter) pan, bring about 3 quarts (2.8 liters) water to a boil over medium-high heat; stir in pasta and cook until just tender to bite, 8 to 10 minutes. (Or cook pasta according to package directions.) Drain well, return to pan, and keep hot.

3. Melt butter in a wide nonstick frying pan over medium heat. Add garlic and cook, stirring, until fragrant (about 30 seconds; do not scorch). Whisk in flour until well blended, then gradually whisk in milk. Cook, whisking constantly, until mixture boils and thickens slightly (about 5 minutes). Whisk in cream cheese, 1 cup (about 3 oz./ 85 g) of the Parmesan cheese, and nutmeg (if desired). Continue to cook, whisking constantly, until cheese is melted and evenly blended into sauce.

4. Working quickly, pour hot sauce over pasta and lift with 2 forks to mix. Spoon pasta into center of 4 shallow individual bowls. Then quickly arrange artichoke mixture around pasta. Sprinkle with remaining ½ cup (40 g) Parmesan cheese, then with pepper. Serve immediately (sauce thickens rapidly and is absorbed quickly by pasta). Makes 4 servings.

....
Per serving: 641 calories (24% calories from fat), 17 g total fat, 9 g saturated fat, 126 mg cholesterol, 924 mg sodium, 82 g carbohydrates, 4 g fiber, 39 g protein, 753 mg calcium, 6 mg iron

---

Simmered in herb-seasoned broth, nutritious lentils make a great topping for linguine.

....

- 1 cup (190 g) lentils
- 2 cups (470 ml) canned vegetable broth
- 1 teaspoon dried thyme
- ⅓ cup (80 ml) lemon juice
- 3 tablespoons chopped fresh basil
- 2 tablespoons (30 ml) olive oil
- 1 teaspoon honey (or to taste)
- 2 cloves garlic, minced
- 12 ounces (340 g) dried linguine
- 1 large tomato (about 8 oz./ 230 g), chopped and drained
- ¾ cup (60 g) grated Parmesan cheese

Linguine with Lentils

....
Preparation time: 20 minutes
Cooking time: About 35 minutes

1. Rinse and sort lentils, discarding any debris; drain lentils. In a 1½- to 2-quart (1.4- to 1.9-liter) pan, bring broth to a boil over high heat; add lentils and thyme. Reduce heat, cover, and simmer just until lentils are tender to bite (25 to 30 minutes). Drain and discard any remaining cooking liquid; keep lentils warm.

2. While lentils are cooking, combine lemon juice, chopped basil, oil, honey, and garlic in a small bowl; set aside. Also bring about 3 quarts (2.8 liters) water to a boil in a 5- to 6-quart (5- to 6-liter) pan over medium-high heat; stir in pasta and cook until just tender to bite, 8 to 10 minutes. (Or cook pasta according to package directions.)

3. Working quickly, drain pasta well and transfer to a large serving bowl. Add basil mixture, lentils, and tomato. Lift with 2 forks to mix. Sprinkle with cheese and serve immediately. Makes 6 servings.

....
Per serving: 426 calories (19% calories from fat), 9 g total fat, 3 g saturated fat, 8 mg cholesterol, 531 mg sodium, 66 g carbohydrates, 5 g fiber, 21 g protein, 185 mg calcium, 6 mg iron

Pungent, mildly bitter greens and butter-toasted pine nuts combine with tender-firm pasta for a satisfying supper dish. Use any favorite pasta shape; we like orecchiette ("little ears").

Orecchiette with Broccoli Rabe & Pine Nuts

Preparation time: 30 minutes
Cooking time: 20 to 25 minutes

- 1 **pound (455 g) broccoli rabe (rapini)**
- 12 **ounces (340 g) dried orecchiette or other medium-size pasta shapes**
- 1 **tablespoon butter**
- 1 **tablespoon (15 ml) olive oil**
- ½ **cup (85 g) finely chopped onion**
- ⅓ **cup (43 g) pine nuts**
- 1 **or 2 small fresh hot red chiles, seeded and thinly sliced**
- 4 **to 6 cloves garlic, minced or pressed**
- 1½ **cups (360 ml) canned vegetable broth**
- 3 **tablespoons chopped Italian or regular parsley**
  Salt

1. Cut off and discard any coarse stem ends from broccoli rabe; discard any bruised or yellow leaves. Rinse and drain broccoli rabe; then cut stems and leaves into 1-inch (2.5-cm) lengths. Leave flowerets whole. Place stems on a steamer rack over about 1 inch of gently boiling water. Cover and steam for 2 to 3 minutes. Add leaves and flowerets; continue to steam until stems are tender-crisp to bite (2 to 3 more minutes). Remove from rack and set aside.

2. In a 5- to 6-quart (5- to 6-liter) pan, bring about 3 quarts (2.8 liters) water to a boil over medium-high heat; stir in pasta and cook until just tender to bite, 8 to 10 minutes.

(Or cook pasta according to package directions.)

3. Meanwhile, melt butter in oil in a wide nonstick frying pan over medium heat. Add onion and pine nuts; cook, stirring often, until onion is translucent but not browned and pine nuts are light golden (about 3 minutes). Add water, 1 tablespoon (15 ml) at a time, if pan appears dry. Add chiles and garlic; cook, stirring often, until fragrant (about 30 seconds; do not scorch). Add all broccoli rabe; cook, stirring often, for 2 minutes. Stir in broth and bring to a boil over medium-high heat. Reduce heat to low and simmer for 1 minute.

4. Working quickly, drain pasta well and transfer to a large serving bowl; top with vegetable mixture. Lift with 2 forks to mix. Sprinkle with parsley; season to taste with salt. Makes 4 servings.

Per serving: 484 calories (26% calories from fat), 14 g total fat, 3 g saturated fat, 8 mg cholesterol, 473 mg sodium, 75 g carbohydrates, 7 g fiber, 18 g protein, 118 mg calcium, 7 mg iron

Great any time of day, this attractive frittata can be served straight from the pan—there's no need for a serving dish.

- 1 teaspoon olive oil
- ½ teaspoon dried rosemary
- 1 pound (455 g) red thin-skinned potatoes, scrubbed and cut into ¼-inch (6-mm) cubes
- 1 small red onion (about 8 oz./230 g), thinly sliced and cut into 1-inch (2.5-cm) slivers
- 4 ounces (115 g) green beans (ends trimmed), cut into 1-inch (2.5-cm) pieces
- ⅓ cup (80 ml) canned vegetable broth
- 1 tablespoon cornstarch
- ¼ teaspoon salt
- 4 large eggs
- 4 large egg whites
- ⅔ cup (60 g) dried cranberries
- ½ cup (55 g) shredded part-skim mozzarella cheese
- 1 large red bell pepper (about 8 oz./230 g), seeded and chopped
- ⅛ teaspoon crushed red pepper flakes (or to taste)

Potato, Green Bean & Bell Pepper Frittata

Preparation time: 25 minutes
Cooking time: About 30 minutes

1. Pour oil into a wide frying pan with an ovenproof handle. Heat oil over medium-high heat; then add rosemary and cook, stirring, just until fragrant (about 30 seconds; do not scorch). Add potatoes, onion, beans, and ½ cup (120 ml) water. Cover, reduce heat to medium, and cook, stirring occasionally, just until potatoes are tender when pierced (about 12 minutes). Add water, about ¼ cup (60 ml) at a time, if pan appears dry.

2. Meanwhile, whisk broth, cornstarch, and salt in a large bowl until smoothly blended. Add eggs and egg whites; whisk until blended. Stir in cranberries and cheese. Set aside.

3. Uncover pan and add half the bell pepper. Cook, stirring, until all liquid has evaporated from vegetable mixture. Whisk egg mixture and pour over vegetables; stir gently to combine. Reduce heat to low; cook until eggs begin to set at pan rim (about 6 minutes). Then broil about 6 inches (15 cm) below heat until frittata feels set when lightly pressed (4 to 6 minutes). Sprinkle with remaining bell pepper and red pepper flakes. Spoon from pan to serve. Makes 4 servings.

Per serving: 329 calories (23% calories from fat), 8 g total fat, 3 g saturated fat, 217 mg cholesterol, 426 mg sodium, 47 g carbohydrates, 5 g fiber, 17 g protein, 170 mg calcium, 2 mg iron

Brilliant red peppers accent this golden combination of polenta, eggs, and cream-style corn in a mildly sweet polenta crust.

⅔ cup (85 g) all-purpose flour

1⅓ cups (183 g) polenta or yellow cornmeal

¼ cup (50 g) sugar

½ teaspoon salt

5 tablespoons (71 g) butter or margarine, cut into chunks

1 jar (about 7 oz./200 g) roasted red peppers, rinsed and patted dry

1 large can (about 15 oz./425 g) cream-style corn

½ cup (120 ml) nonfat sour cream

1 large egg

5 large egg whites

2 tablespoons cornstarch

¼ cup (28 g) shredded fontina or mozzarella cheese

1 tablespoon chopped fresh oregano or 1 teaspoon dried oregano

Oregano sprigs

Polenta Pepper Torte

Preparation time: 25 minutes
Cooking time: About 1 hour
Pictured on facing page

1. In a food processor or a large bowl, whirl or stir together flour, ⅔ cup (92 g) of the polenta, sugar, and ¼ teaspoon of the salt. Add butter and 1 tablespoon (15 ml) water; whirl or rub together with your fingers until mixture resembles coarse crumbs. If pastry is too dry, add a little more water.

2. Press pastry firmly over bottom and about 1 inch (2.5 cm) up sides of a 9-inch (23-cm) nonstick or well-greased regular cheesecake pan with a removable rim. Prick all over with a fork to prevent puffing. Bake in a 350°F (175°C) oven until crust is tinged with gold and feels slightly firmer when pressed (about 15 minutes). Let cool on a rack for 5 minutes.

3. Cut any very large pieces of red peppers into smaller pieces. Arrange peppers in baked crust. In food processor, whirl remaining ⅔ cup (92 g) polenta, corn, sour cream, egg, egg whites, cornstarch, and remaining ¼ teaspoon salt until smooth. Pour egg mixture over peppers in crust. Sprinkle with cheese.

4. Return torte to oven and bake until filling is golden and a knife inserted in center comes out clean (about 45 minutes). Let cool on a rack for about 10 minutes. To serve, sprinkle with chopped oregano and garnish with oregano sprigs. Remove pan rim; then cut torte into wedges with a very sharp knife. Makes 6 servings.

Per serving: 498 calories (28% calories from fat), 15 g total fat, 9 g saturated fat, 80 mg cholesterol, 809 mg sodium, 76 g carbohydrates, 3 g fiber, 14 g protein, 65 mg calcium, 3 mg iron

Polenta Pepper Torte
(recipe on facing page)

Polenta Berry Muffins

Preparation time: 15 minutes
Cooking time: 20 to 25 minutes

....

- 1 cup (125 g) all-purpose flour
- 1 cup (138 g) polenta or yellow cornmeal
- 2 tablespoons sugar
- 1 teaspoon baking powder
- ¼ teaspoon salt
- 1 large egg
- 1 cup (240 ml) low-fat (2%) milk
- 1 tablespoon butter or margarine, melted
- 1 cup (123 g) fresh raspberries or blueberries

....

1. In a large bowl, stir together flour, polenta, sugar, baking powder, and salt. In a medium-size bowl, beat egg, milk, and butter to blend. Add egg mixture to flour mixture; stir just until dry ingredients are evenly moistened. Gently mix in berries.

2. Spoon batter equally into 12 lightly oiled 2½-inch (6-cm) nonstick or regular muffin cups. Bake in a 425°F (220°C) oven until muffins are brown (20 to 25 minutes). Let cool in pans on a rack for about 5 minutes, then turn out of pans and serve warm. Makes 12 muffins.

Per muffin: 123 calories (19% calories from fat), 3 g total fat, 1 g saturated fat, 22 mg cholesterol, 111 mg sodium, 21 g carbohydrates, 1 g fiber, 3 g protein, 54 mg calcium, 1 mg iron

Mushroom, Ham & Cheese Calzones

Preparation time: 25 minutes
Cooking time: About 35 minutes

....

- 5 to 6 ounces (140 to 170 g) mushrooms, sliced
- 1 very large onion (about 10 oz./285 g), thinly sliced
- 2 cloves garlic, minced
- 2 tablespoons minced fresh basil or 2 teaspoons dried basil
- ½ cup (120 ml) fat-free reduced-sodium chicken broth
- 1 tablespoon all-purpose flour
- 2 cups (280 g) chopped cooked ham
- 1 loaf (about 1 lb./455 g) frozen white bread dough, thawed
- ¾ cup (85 g) shredded fontina cheese
- 1 large egg yolk beaten with 1 tablespoon (15 ml) water

....

1. In a wide frying pan, combine mushrooms, onion, garlic, basil, and ¼ cup (60 ml) of the broth. Cook over medium-high heat, stirring often, until vegetables brown and begin to stick to pan bottom (about 8 minutes). To deglaze pan, stir in remaining ¼ cup (60 ml) broth and stir to scrape browned bits free from pan bottom. Continue to cook, stirring, until almost all liquid has evaporated. Stir in flour and ham; remove from heat.

2. On a lightly floured board, divide dough into 4 equal pieces; shape each into a ball. To shape each calzone, roll one ball into a 5- to 6-inch (12.5- to 15-cm) round; then flatten it with your hands until it is 7 to 8 inches (18 to 20 cm) in diameter.

3. Spoon a fourth of the ham filling over half each round, spreading it to within ½ inch (1 cm) of edge. Sprinkle filling with a fourth of the cheese. Brush edge of dough round with water; fold plain half of round over filling and press edges firmly together to seal. With a fork, prick top several times.

4. Transfer calzones to a lightly oiled 12- by 15-inch (30- by 38-cm) baking sheet. Brush with egg yolk mixture. Bake in a 425°F (220°C) oven until richly browned (about 20 minutes). Let cool slightly before serving. Makes 4 servings.

Per serving: 571 calories (30% calories from fat), 19 g total fat, 7 g saturated fat, 12 mg cholesterol, 1,656 mg sodium, 67 g carbohydrates, 2 g fiber, 32 g protein, 201 mg calcium, 4 mg iron

Breakfast Bruschetta

Preparation time: 20 minutes
Cooking time: About 5 minutes

....

- ¼ cup (25 g) chopped dried apricots
- 3 tablespoons (45 ml) fresh orange juice
- 8 slices crusty bread, such as Italian ciabatta or French bread (about 8 oz./230 g *total*)
- 2 cups (246 g) mixed fresh berries, such as raspberries, blueberries, and blackberries
- 1 tablespoon chopped fresh mint

  About 1 teaspoon sugar (or to taste)
- 1 cup (about 8 oz./230 g) nonfat ricotta cheese
- 3 tablespoons (45 ml) honey
- ½ teaspoon ground coriander

....

1. In a small bowl, soak apricots in orange juice until soft (about 10 minutes), stirring occasionally.

2. Meanwhile, arrange bread slices slightly apart in a shallow 10- by 15-inch (25- by 38-cm) baking pan. Broil about 6 inches (15 cm) below heat, turning once, until golden on both sides (about 5 minutes). Let cool on a rack.

3. In a medium-size bowl, combine berries, mint, and sugar; mix gently and set aside. In a food processor or blender, combine apricot mixture, ricotta cheese, honey, and coriander; whirl until smoothly blended.

4. Top toast slices equally with ricotta mixture, then berries. Makes 4 servings.

Per serving: 322 calories (6% calories from fat), 2 g total fat, 0.5 g saturated fat, 5 mg cholesterol, 389 mg sodium, 62 g carbohydrates, 5 g fiber, 15 g protein, 357 mg calcium, 2 mg iron

Ricotta Pancakes with Lemon-Maple Syrup

Preparation time: 20 minutes
Cooking time: 10 to 15 minutes

½ **cup (120 ml) pure maple syrup**

½ **teaspoon grated lemon peel**

1 **teaspoon lemon juice**

2 **large eggs**

⅔ **cup (152 g) nonfat ricotta cheese**

¼ **cup (50 g) sugar**

¼ **cup (60 ml) half-and-half**

1 **teaspoon vanilla**

½ **cup (60 g) all-purpose flour**

¼ **teaspoon baking powder**

2 **large egg whites**

¼ **teaspoon cream of tartar**

⅛ **teaspoon salt**

2 **tablespoons (30 ml) salad oil**

1. In a small pan, combine syrup, ¼ teaspoon of the lemon peel, and lemon juice. Stir over medium heat until steaming (3 to 5 minutes); keep warm over very low heat.

2. In a food processor or blender, combine eggs, ricotta cheese, 2 tablespoons of the sugar, half-and-half, vanilla, and remaining ¼ teaspoon lemon peel; whirl until smooth. Add flour and baking powder; whirl until flour is evenly moistened. Transfer batter to a medium-size bowl.

3. In a large, deep bowl, beat egg whites and 1 tablespoon (15 ml) water with an electric mixer on high speed until frothy. Beat in cream of tartar and salt. Add remaining 2 tablespoons sugar, 1 tablespoon at a time, beating until mixture holds stiff, moist peaks. Stir about a third of the egg white mixture into batter to lighten it; then fold batter into remaining egg white mixture.

4. Heat 1 tablespoon (15 ml) of the oil on each of 2 nonstick griddles over medium heat (or heat oil in wide nonstick frying pans). For each pancake, measure out ⅓ cup (80 ml) batter, scooping it up from bottom of bowl; pour onto griddle and spread out slightly. Cook until tops of pancakes are bubbly and almost dry (2 to 3 minutes); turn over and cook until browned on bottoms (about 2 more minutes). Serve with warm syrup. Makes about 12 pancakes (4 servings).

Per serving: 379 calories (27% calories from fat), 11 g total fat, 3 g saturated fat, 115 mg cholesterol, 209 mg sodium, 56 g carbohydrates, 0.4 g fiber, 14 g protein, 289 mg calcium, 2 mg iron

Orange Polenta Cakes

Preparation time: 20 minutes
Cooking time: About 20 minutes

½ **teaspoon grated orange peel**

2½ **cups (590 ml) fresh orange juice**

½ **teaspoon salt**

1 **cup (138 g) polenta or yellow cornmeal**

2 **tablespoons butter or margarine**

About ¼ cup (60 ml) honey

½ **cup (60 g) slivered almonds**

1½ **cups (360 ml) plain nonfat yogurt**

About 2 cups (330 g) sliced fresh fruit

1. In a 2- to 2½-quart (1.9- to 2.4-liter) pan, bring orange peel, orange juice, and salt to a boil over medium-high heat.

Gradually add polenta, stirring until blended. Reduce heat and boil gently, uncovered, stirring often and scraping bottom of pan with a long-handled spoon (mixture will spatter), until polenta is thick (about 10 minutes). Reduce heat to low; continue to stir until polenta stops flowing after spoon is drawn across pan bottom (3 to 5 more minutes). Stir in butter and ¼ cup (60 ml) of the honey.

2. Divide hot polenta among 4 greased ¾-cup (180-ml) custard cups; with the back of a spoon, press polenta solidly into cups. Let cool for at least 5 minutes or up to 30 minutes.

3. Meanwhile, toast almonds in a wide frying pan over medium heat until golden (about 3 minutes), stirring often. Pour out of pan and set aside. Sweeten yogurt to taste with honey.

4. To serve, run a knife around edge of each cup; invert polenta cakes onto individual plates. Sprinkle cakes with almonds; accompany with sweetened yogurt and fruit. Makes 4 servings.

Per serving: 522 calories (26% calories from fat), 16 g total fat, 5 g saturated fat, 17 mg cholesterol, 402 mg sodium, 87 g carbohydrates, 5 g fiber, 13 g protein, 258 mg calcium, 3 mg iron

Tiramisu
(recipe on page 80)

Desserts

Indulge yourself—enjoy one of our low-fat desserts! Espresso Cheesecake, Pistachio Ice Cream, and Amaretto Soufflé are all as rich and sweet as you could wish, perfect conclusions to your lean Italian meals. For other fitting finales, try our fruit specialties, from simple poached pears to an apricot-studded almond torte to an unusual tart filled with tender sliced apples, currants, and fennel.

•

A perfect partner for hot coffee at any time of day, popular tiramisu features a filling of sweet, creamy cheese spooned over ladyfingers soaked in brandy and espresso. Garnish the dessert with chocolate curls and a dusting of cocoa before serving.

....

- 20 **ladyfingers (about 5 oz./140 g total)**
- ⅔ **cup (67 g) sifted powdered sugar**
- 6 **ounces (170 g) nonfat cream cheese, at room temperature**
- 2 **ounces (55 g) mascarpone cheese, at room temperature**
- 2 **cups (470 ml) frozen reduced-calorie whipped topping, thawed**
- 9 **tablespoons (108 g) granulated sugar**
- 3 **large egg whites**
- ¼ **teaspoon cream of tartar**
- 1 **tablespoon instant espresso powder**
- 2 **tablespoons (30 ml) brandy, coffee-flavored liqueur, or orange juice**

  About 2 tablespoons unsweetened cocoa powder

  Semisweet chocolate curls

Tiramisu

....

Preparation time: 25 minutes
Cooking time: About 5 minutes
Chilling time: At least 3 hours
Pictured on page 78

1. Split ladyfingers into halves. Arrange half the ladyfinger halves, cut side up, over bottom of an 8-inch-square (20-cm-square) dish or pan; overlap ladyfingers as needed to fit. Set aside.

2. In a food processor or a large bowl, combine powdered sugar, cream cheese, and mascarpone cheese. Whirl or beat with an electric mixer until smooth. Gently fold in 1 cup (240 ml) of the whipped topping; cover and refrigerate.

3. In a large metal bowl, combine ½ cup (100 g) of the granulated sugar, ¼ cup (60 ml) water, egg whites, and cream of tartar. Beat with an electric mixer on low speed until foamy. Nest bowl over a pan of simmering water (do not let bowl touch water) and beat on high speed until mixture holds stiff peaks. Lift bowl from pan; stir about a fourth of the egg white mixture into cheese mix-

ture to lighten it, then gently but thoroughly fold in remaining egg white mixture. Set aside.

4. Working quickly, stir together ½ cup (120 ml) hot water, remaining 1 tablespoon sugar, instant espresso, and brandy in a small bowl. Drizzle half the hot espresso mixture evenly over ladyfingers in dish. Top with half the cheese mixture, spreading mixture level. Top with remaining ladyfinger halves (cut side up), espresso mixture, and cheese mixture. Cover with remaining 1 cup (240 ml) whipped topping and smooth top.

5. Cover dessert airtight (do not let cover touch topping) and refrigerate until cold (at least 3 hours) or until next day. Spoon out of dish or cut to serve. Sift cocoa over individual servings and garnish with chocolate curls. Makes 8 servings.

....

Per serving: 261 calories (25% calories from fat), 7 g total fat, 3 g saturated fat, 77 mg cholesterol, 153 mg sodium, 40 g carbohydrates, 0.3 g fiber, 7 g protein, 71 mg calcium, 0.8 mg iron

Chocolate Hazelnut Cake

Preparation time: 25 minutes
Cooking time: About 15 minutes
Chilling time: At least 2 hours

Filled with smooth, luscious hazelnut spread and topped with chocolate–cream cheese frosting, this fancy dessert gets a quick start with a purchased loaf cake.

- 2 tablespoons hazelnuts
- 1 purchased nonfat chocolate loaf cake (about 15 oz./425 g)
- ½ cup (120 ml) purchased hazelnut-cocoa spread
- 1 small package (about 6 oz./ 170 g) semisweet chocolate chips
- 2 cups (200 g) sifted powdered sugar
- 1 large package (about 8 oz./ 230 g) Neufchâtel cheese, cut into chunks
- ½ cup (43 g) unsweetened cocoa powder
- ¼ cup (60 ml) nonfat sour cream
- 2 teaspoons vanilla

1. Toast and coarsely chop hazelnuts as directed for Espresso Biscotti (page 92). Set aside.

2. Cut cake in half horizontally. Set bottom half, cut side up, on a serving plate. Stir hazelnut-cocoa spread to soften, if necessary; then spread evenly over cake to within about ½ inch (1 cm) of edges. Place top half of cake, cut side down, over filling; press lightly.

3. Place chocolate chips in a metal bowl nested over a pan of hot (not boiling) water. Stir often until chocolate is melted and smooth. Remove from heat and transfer to a food processor or blender; let stand for 2 to 3 minutes to cool slightly. Add powdered sugar, Neufchâtel cheese, cocoa, sour cream, and vanilla; whirl until smooth, scraping sides of container often. Let frosting cool slightly; it should be spreadable, but not too soft.

4. Generously spread frosting over sides and top of cake. Cover cake with a cake cover or an inverted bowl (don't let cover touch frosting); refrigerate until cold (at least 2 hours) or until next day. Sprinkle with hazelnuts, pressing them lightly into frosting. Cut into slices to serve. Makes 10 servings.

Per serving: 401 calories (29% calories from fat), 13 g total fat, 6 g saturated fat, 11 mg cholesterol, 324 mg sodium, 67 g carbohydrates, 2 g fiber, 7 g protein, 66 mg calcium, 2 mg iron

Anise Poofs

Preparation time: 25 minutes
Standing time: 8 to 24 hours
Cooking time: About 8 minutes

A touch of olive oil enriches this easy make-ahead dough. Serve the delicate anise-flavored cookies with milk, coffee, or sweet dessert wine.

- About 2 cups (200 g) sifted powdered sugar
- 1 cup (125 g) all-purpose flour
- 1 teaspoon baking powder
- ¼ teaspoon ground cinnamon
- 1 tablespoon (15 ml) olive oil
- 1 large egg, beaten
- 2 tablespoons (30 ml) anisette liqueur; or 1 teaspoon anise extract (or to taste) blended with 5 teaspoons (25 ml) water
- 1 teaspoon vanilla

1. In a large bowl, stir together 2 cups (200 g) of the powdered sugar, flour, baking powder, and cinnamon. Add oil, egg, liqueur, and vanilla; stir until well blended. Turn dough out onto a board lightly dusted with powdered sugar; knead until smooth, about 4 turns.

2. Cut dough into 6 pieces. Roll each piece into a rope 20 inches (50 cm) long and about ½ inch (1 cm) wide. Cut each rope into 2-inch (5-cm) lengths. Place pieces about 1½ inches (3.5 cm) apart on lightly oiled large baking sheets. Let cookies stand, uncovered, for 8 to 24 hours. (*Do not* omit standing time; if dough does not stand, cookies will not puff.) Then bake in a 325°F (165°C) oven until pale golden (about 8 minutes). Immediately transfer cookies to racks and let cool. Makes 5 dozen cookies.

Per cookie: 27 calories (18% calories from fat), 0.5 g total fat, 0.1 g saturated fat, 4 mg cholesterol, 9 mg sodium, 5 g carbohydrates, 0 g fiber, 0.3 g protein, 5 mg calcium, 0.1 mg iron

Tender almond-flavored cake studded with sliced fresh apricots makes a pretty company dessert. Serve it with a silky, orange-accented apricot sauce.

- 1 tablespoon (15 ml) lemon juice
- 5 medium-size apricots (about 1 lb./455 g *total*)
- ¼ cup (30 g) slivered almonds
- 2 large eggs
- 1 cup (200 g) sugar
- 4 to 5 tablespoons (60 to 75 ml) almond-flavored liqueur
- ½ teaspoon almond extract
- ¾ cup (95 g) all-purpose flour
- 2 teaspoons baking powder
- ⅛ teaspoon salt
- ¼ cup (55 g) butter or margarine, melted and cooled slightly
- 4 teaspoons cornstarch
- 1 cup (240 ml) apricot nectar
- ½ cup (120 ml) fresh orange juice
- ½ teaspoon vanilla

Apricot-Amaretto Torte

Preparation time: 25 minutes
Cooking time: About 25 minutes
Pictured on facing page

1. Pour lemon juice into a medium-size bowl. Quarter and pit apricots; add to bowl and turn to coat with juice. Set aside.

2. In a food processor, whirl almonds until finely ground. (Or finely chop almonds with a knife, then place in a large bowl.) To almonds, add eggs, ½ cup (100 g) of the sugar, 1 tablespoon (15 ml) of the liqueur, and almond extract; whirl or beat with an electric mixer until thick and well blended. Add flour, baking powder, salt, and butter; whirl or beat until well blended. Spread batter in a greased, floured 9-inch (23-cm) cake pan with a removable rim. Decoratively arrange apricots in batter, overlap-

ping as needed; press fruit lightly into batter.

3. Bake in a 375°F (190°C) oven until cake just begins to pull away from side of pan and a wooden pick inserted in center comes out clean (about 25 minutes; pierce cake, not fruit). Let cool slightly on a rack.

4. While cake is cooling, stir together cornstarch and 6 tablespoons (72 g) of the sugar in a small pan. Whisk in apricot nectar and orange juice; cook over medium-high heat, whisking constantly, until mixture boils and thickens slightly (about 2 minutes). Remove from heat and stir in vanilla and remaining 3 to 4 tablespoons (45 to 60 ml) liqueur; keep warm.

5. Sprinkle cake with remaining 2 tablespoons sugar. Remove pan rim and cut cake into wedges; serve with apricot-orange sauce. Makes 8 servings.

Per serving: 340 calories (28% calories from fat), 10 g total fat, 4 g saturated fat, 69 mg cholesterol, 240 mg sodium, 54 g carbohydrates, 1 g fiber, 5 g protein, 100 mg calcium, 1 mg iron

Apricot-Amaretto Torte
(recipe on facing page)

Biscotti

Lemon Poppy Seed Biscotti

Preparation time: 25 minutes
Cooking time: About 25 minutes

- 5 tablespoons (71 g) butter or margarine, at room temperature
- ½ cup (100 g) granulated sugar
- 2 teaspoons grated lemon peel
- 2 large eggs
- 1 teaspoon vanilla
- 2 tablespoons poppy seeds
- 2 cups (250 g) all-purpose flour
- 2 teaspoons baking powder
- 1½ cups (150 g) sifted powdered sugar
- About 5 teaspoons (25 ml) lemon juice

1. In a large bowl, beat butter, granulated sugar, and 1½ teaspoons of the lemon peel until well blended. Add eggs, one at a time, beating well after each addition. Stir in vanilla; then mix in poppy seeds. In a medium-size bowl, stir together flour and baking powder; add to butter mixture and stir until well blended.

2. Divide dough in half. On a lightly floured board, shape each portion into a long roll about 1½ inches (3.5 cm) in diameter. Place rolls on a large nonstick or greased regular baking sheet, spacing them 3 inches (8 cm) apart. Flatten rolls to make ½-inch-thick (1-cm-thick) loaves. Bake in a 350°F (175°C) oven until loaves feel firm to the touch (about 15 minutes).

3. Remove baking sheet from oven and let loaves cool for 3 to 5 minutes; then cut crosswise into slices about ½ inch (1 cm) thick. Tip slices cut side down on baking sheet (at this point, you may need another sheet to bake biscotti all at once). Return to oven and continue to bake until biscotti look dry and are lightly browned (about 10 minutes); if using 2 baking sheets, switch their positions halfway through baking. Transfer biscotti to racks and let cool.

4. Meanwhile, in a small bowl, combine powdered sugar, remaining ½ teaspoon lemon peel, and 5 teaspoons (25 ml) of the lemon juice; stir until icing is easy to spread, adding a little more lemon juice as needed.

5. Spread icing over about 1½ inches (3.5 cm) of one end of each cooled cookie. Let stand until icing is firm before serving. Makes about 3½ dozen cookies.

Per cookie: 66 calories (28% calories from fat), 2 g total fat, 1 g saturated fat, 14 mg cholesterol, 43 mg sodium, 11 g carbohydrates, 0.2 g fiber, 1 g protein, 22 mg calcium, 0.3 mg iron

Cornmeal–Pine Nut Biscotti

Preparation time: 30 minutes
Cooking time: About 35 minutes

- 2 tablespoons butter or margarine, at room temperature
- ¼ cup (50 g) sugar
- 1 teaspoon fennel seeds
- 2 teaspoons dry sherry or water
- 2 large egg whites
- ¾ cup (95 g) all-purpose flour
- ⅓ cup (45 g) yellow cornmeal
- 1 tablespoon cornstarch
- ½ teaspoon baking powder
- 2 to 3 tablespoons pine nuts

1. In a large bowl, beat butter, sugar, fennel seeds, and sherry until well blended. Add egg whites and beat until well blended. In a small bowl, stir together flour, cornmeal, cornstarch, and baking powder; add to butter mixture and stir until well blended. Mix in pine nuts. Dough will be soft.

2. Scrape dough out onto a large nonstick or greased regular baking sheet. With heavily floured fingers, shape dough into a loaf about 15 inches (38 cm) long and 1½ inches (3.5 cm) in diameter. Bake in a 375°F (190°C) oven until loaf feels firm to the touch (about 20 minutes).

3. Remove baking sheet from oven and let loaf cool for 3 to 5 minutes; then cut crosswise into slices about ½ inch (1 cm) thick. Tip slices cut side down on baking sheet (at this point, you may need another sheet to bake biscotti all at once).

4. Reduce oven temperature to 350°F (175°C). Return baking sheet(s) to oven and continue to bake until biscotti look dry and are lightly browned (about 15 minutes); if using 2 baking sheets, switch their positions halfway through baking. Transfer biscotti to racks and let cool. Makes about 2 dozen cookies.

Per cookie: 46 calories (29% calories from fat), 1 g total fat, 0.7 g saturated fat, 3 mg cholesterol, 25 mg sodium, 7 g carbohydrates, 0.3 g fiber, 1 g protein, 8 mg calcium, 0.4 mg iron

Anise Biscotti

Preparation time: 25 minutes
Cooking time: About 25 minutes

- 5 tablespoons (71 g) butter or margarine, at room temperature
- 11 tablespoons (132 g) sugar
- 1½ teaspoons anise seeds (or to taste)
- 2 large eggs
- 2 teaspoons vanilla
- 2 cups (250 g) all-purpose flour
- 2 teaspoons baking powder
- 2 large egg whites

1. In a large bowl, beat butter, ½ cup (100 g) of the sugar, and anise seeds until well blended. Add eggs, one at a time, beating well after each addition. Stir in vanilla. In a medium-size bowl, stir together flour and baking powder; add to butter mixture and stir until well blended.

2. Divide dough in half. On a lightly floured board, shape each portion into a long roll about 1½ inches (3.5 cm) in diameter. Place rolls on a large nonstick or greased regular baking sheet, spacing them 3 inches (8 cm) apart. Flatten rolls to make ½-inch-thick (1-cm-thick) loaves.

3. In a small bowl, whisk egg whites with 1 tablespoon (15 ml) water until blended; brush some of the mixture lightly over loaves. Bake in a 350°F (175°C) oven until loaves feel firm to the touch (about 15 minutes).

4. Remove baking sheet from oven and let loaves cool for 3 to 5 minutes; then cut crosswise into slices about ½ inch (1 cm) thick. Tip slices cut side down on baking sheet (at this point, you may need another sheet to bake biscotti all at once). Brush slices with remaining egg white mixture and sprinkle with remaining 3 tablespoons sugar.

5. Return to oven and bake until biscotti look dry and are lightly browned (about 10 minutes); if using 2 baking sheets, switch their positions halfway through baking. Transfer biscotti to racks and let cool. Makes about 4 dozen cookies.

Per cookie: 45 calories (29% calories from fat), 1 g total fat, 0.8 g saturated fat, 12 mg cholesterol, 38 mg sodium, 7 g carbohydrates, 0.1 g fiber, 0.9 g protein, 14 mg calcium, 0.3 mg iron

Chocolate Biscotti

Preparation time: 25 minutes
Cooking time: 35 to 40 minutes

- ¼ cup (55 g) butter or margarine, at room temperature
- ½ cup (100 g) granulated sugar
- 4 large egg whites
- 2 cups (250 g) all-purpose flour
- ⅓ cup (29 g) unsweetened cocoa powder
- 2 teaspoons baking powder
- ⅓ cup (33 g) sifted powdered sugar
- About 2 teaspoons low-fat (1%) milk

1. In a large bowl, beat butter and granulated sugar until fluffy. Add egg whites and beat until well blended. In a medium-size bowl, stir together flour, cocoa, and baking powder; add to butter mixture and stir until well blended.

2. Turn dough out onto a large nonstick or lightly greased regular baking sheet. Shape dough down length of sheet into a loaf about 2½ inches (6 cm) wide and ⅝ inch (2 cm) thick. Bake in a 350°F (175°C) oven until crusty and firm to the touch (about 20 minutes).

3. Remove baking sheet from oven and let loaf cool for 3 to 5 minutes; then cut diagonally into slices about ½ inch (1 cm) thick. Tip slices cut side down on baking sheet. Return to oven and continue to bake until biscotti feel firm and dry (15 to 20 minutes). Transfer to racks and let cool.

4. In a small bowl, stir together powdered sugar and 2 teaspoons of the milk, or enough to make a pourable icing. Using a spoon, drizzle icing decoratively over biscotti. Let stand until icing is firm before serving. Makes about 1½ dozen cookies.

Per cookie: 112 calories (25% calories from fat), 3 g total fat, 2 g saturated fat, 7 mg cholesterol, 97 mg sodium, 19 g carbohydrates, 0.8 g fiber, 3 g protein, 36 mg calcium, 0.9 mg iron

Port Ice
(recipe on facing page)

For a cooling conclusion to a special meal, serve a simple, vividly colored ice made from a blend of port wine, orange juice, and aromatic bitters.

- ½ cup (100 g) sugar
- 1 cup (240 ml) port or cream sherry
- ¼ cup (60 ml) fresh orange juice
- 1 teaspoon aromatic bitters

1. In a 1- to 2-quart (950-ml to 1.9-liter) pan, combine sugar and 1½ cups (360 ml) water. Bring to a boil

Port Ice

Preparation time: 10 minutes
Cooking time: About 5 minutes
Chilling & freezing time: About 5 hours
Pictured on facing page

over high heat, stirring until sugar is dissolved. Remove from heat and let cool; then stir in port, orange juice, and bitters. Cover and refrigerate until cold (about 1 hour).

2. Pour port mixture into a metal pan 8 to 9 inches (20 to 23 cm)

square; cover and freeze until solid (about 4 hours) or for up to 3 days.

3. To serve, break mixture into chunks with a heavy spoon, transfer to a blender or food processor, and whirl until slushy; then spoon into bowls and serve at once. (Or pour cold port mixture into container of a self-refrigerated ice cream machine and freeze according to manufacturer's instructions.) Makes 6 to 8 servings.

Per serving: 114 calories (0% calories from fat), 0 g total fat, 0 g saturated fat, 0 mg cholesterol, 3 mg sodium, 19 g carbohydrates, 0 g fiber, 0.1 g protein, 4 mg calcium, 0.1 mg iron

---

Smooth, creamy, and studded with pistachios, this easy ice cream is sure to be a family favorite.

- 2 jars (about 7 oz./200 g *each*) marshmallow fluff (marshmallow creme)
- 1 large package (about 8 oz./ 230 g) Neufchâtel cheese, at room temperature
- ½ cup (120 ml) low-fat buttermilk
- 2 teaspoons vanilla
- 1 large carton (about 1 lb./ 455 g) nonfat sour cream
- ½ cup (60 g) shelled salted roasted pistachio nuts

Pistachio Ice Cream

Preparation time: 15 minutes
Chilling time: About 1 hour
Freezing time: Depends on ice cream machine

1. In a food processor or blender, combine marshmallow fluff, Neufchâtel cheese, buttermilk, and vanilla. Whirl until smooth. Stir in sour cream.

2. Transfer mixture to a large bowl; cover and refrigerate until cold

(about 1 hour) or until next day. Stir in pistachios.

3. Transfer mixture to container of a self-refrigerated ice cream machine and freeze according to manufacturer's instructions. Makes about 12 servings.

Per serving: 217 calories (30% calories from fat), 7 g total fat, 3 g saturated fat, 15 mg cholesterol, 146 mg sodium, 32 g carbohydrates, 0 g fiber, 7 g protein, 85 mg calcium, 0.5 mg iron

Campari Ice

Preparation time: 10 minutes
Cooking time: About 5 minutes
Chilling & freezing time: About 5 hours

This refreshing ice of sweet vermouth and astringent Campari is a welcome hot-weather dessert—or an unusual starter for a special meal.

- ½ cup (100 g) sugar
- 1 cup (240 ml) sweet vermouth or fresh orange juice
- 2 tablespoons (30 ml) Campari or 2 teaspoons aromatic bitters
- 1 tablespoon (15 ml) lime juice
  Thin lime slices

1. In a 1- to 2-quart (950-ml to 1.9-liter) pan, combine sugar and 1½ cups (360 ml) water. Bring to a boil over high heat, stirring until sugar is dissolved. Remove from heat and let cool; then stir in vermouth, Campari, and lime juice. Cover mixture and refrigerate until cold (about 1 hour).

2. Pour mixture into a metal pan 8 to 9 inches (20 to 23 cm) square; cover and freeze until solid (about 4 hours) or for up to 3 days.

3. To serve, break mixture into chunks with a heavy spoon, transfer to a blender or food processor, and whirl until slushy; then spoon into bowls and serve at once. (Or pour cold port mixture into container of a self-refrigerated ice cream machine and freeze according to manufacturer's instructions.) Garnish individual servings with lime slices. Makes 6 to 8 servings.

Per serving: 120 calories (0% calories from fat), 0 g total fat, 0 g saturated fat, 0 mg cholesterol, 4 mg sodium, 20 g carbohydrates, 0 g fiber, 0 g protein, 3 mg calcium, 0.1 mg iron

Amaretto Soufflé

Preparation time: 25 minutes
Cooking time: About 35 minutes

This soufflé owes its intense almond flavor to crushed amaretti cookies, amaretto liqueur, and almond extract.

- ½ cup (64 g) coarsely crushed amaretti cookies (about ten 1½-inch/4-cm cookies)
- ¾ cup (180 ml) low-fat (2%) milk
- 3 large egg yolks
- 6 tablespoons (72 g) granulated sugar
- ¼ cup (30 g) all-purpose flour
- ¼ cup (60 ml) almond-flavored or other nut-flavored liqueur
- ⅛ teaspoon almond extract
- 5 large egg whites
- ½ teaspoon cream of tartar
- ⅛ teaspoon salt
  About 1 tablespoon sifted powdered sugar

1. Sprinkle crushed cookies over bottom of a greased 1½- to 1¾-quart (1.4- to 1.7-liter) soufflé dish. Place dish in a larger pan (at least 2 inches/5 cm deep); set aside.

2. Bring milk to a boil in a medium-size nonstick pan over medium heat (about 5 minutes), stirring often. Remove from heat and let cool slightly.

3. In a large bowl, whisk egg yolks and 3 tablespoons of the granulated sugar until thick and lemon-colored. Add flour and whisk until smoothly blended. Whisk in a little of the warm milk, then whisk egg yolk mixture back into warm milk in pan. Return to heat and stir constantly (be careful not to scratch pan) just until mixture boils and thickens slightly. Return to large bowl and whisk in liqueur and almond extract; let cool completely.

4. In a clean large, deep bowl, beat egg whites and 1 tablespoon (15 ml) water with an electric mixer on high speed until frothy. Beat in cream of tartar and salt. Then beat in remaining 3 tablespoons granulated sugar, 1 tablespoon at a time; continue to beat until mixture holds stiff, moist peaks. Stir about a third of the egg white mixture into yolk mixture; then fold all of yolk mixture into egg white mixture.

5. Gently spoon soufflé batter into prepared dish. Set pan with dish on middle rack of a 350°F (175°C) oven. Pour boiling water into larger pan up to level of soufflé batter. Bake until soufflé is richly browned and center jiggles only slightly when dish is gently shaken (about 25 minutes); if top begins to brown excessively, carefully cover dish with foil. As soon as soufflé is done, sprinkle it with powdered sugar and serve immediately. Makes 6 servings.

Per serving: 198 calories (21% calories from fat), 4 g total fat, 1 g saturated fat, 109 mg cholesterol, 115 mg sodium, 29 g carbohydrates, 0.1 g fiber, 6 g protein, 51 mg calcium, 0.5 mg iron

Poached Pears with Ruby Citrus Syrup

Preparation time: 15 minutes
Cooking time: 30 to 45 minutes

Here's a lovely autumn dessert: poached whole pears served in a glistening port-citrus syrup spiced with nutmeg.

- 2 cups (470 ml) port
- ½ cup (100 g) sugar
- 1 tablespoon shredded orange peel
- ¼ teaspoon ground nutmeg
- 4 large firm-ripe pears (about 2 lbs./905 g *total*)
- 1 tablespoon (15 ml) lemon juice
- 2 teaspoons finely shredded orange peel

1. In a 3- to 4-quart (2.8- to 3.8-liter) pan, combine port, sugar, the 1 tablespoon orange peel, and nutmeg. Stir over medium heat until sugar is dissolved; then bring to a boil, stirring often.

2. Add whole pears to hot syrup. Reduce heat, cover, and simmer until pears are very tender when pierced (20 to 30 minutes), turning fruit over a few times. With a slotted spoon, transfer pears to a wide bowl or rimmed platter; set aside.

3. Bring cooking liquid to a boil over high heat; then boil, uncovered, until liquid is thickened and reduced to about ½ cup (120 ml), 10 to 12 minutes. Stir in lemon juice; then pour syrup over pears. Garnish with the 2 teaspoons orange peel. Serve warm or at room temperature. Makes 4 servings.

Per serving: 282 calories (3% calories from fat), 0.9 g total fat, 0.1 g saturated fat, 0 mg cholesterol, 12 mg sodium, 72 g carbohydrates, 5 g fiber, 1 g protein, 38 mg calcium, 0.8 mg iron

Zabaglione Cream over Warm Fruit Compote

Preparation time: 15 minutes
Cooking time: About 40 minutes

For a luxurious dessert, stir a hot froth of Marsala wine, sugar, and egg yolks into whipped topping; then spoon over poached dried fruits.

- 1 package (about 12 oz./340 g) mixed dried fruit (whole or halved fruits, not dried fruit bits)
- 1½ cups (360 ml) white grape juice
- ¼ to ½ teaspoon ground cinnamon
- 3 whole cloves
- 6 large egg yolks
- 3 tablespoons sugar
- ½ cup (120 ml) Marsala
- 2 cups (470 ml) frozen reduced-calorie whipped topping, thawed

1. Cut large pieces of fruit into bite-size chunks; set fruit aside. In a medium-size pan, combine grape juice, cinnamon, and cloves; bring to a boil over high heat. Stir in fruit; then reduce heat, cover, and simmer until fruit is plump and tender when pierced (about 30 minutes). Remove from heat and keep warm.

2. In the top of a double boiler, combine egg yolks and sugar. Beat with an electric mixer on high speed or with a whisk until thick and lemon-colored. Beat in Marsala. Set double boiler over (not in) gently simmering water; beat mixture constantly just until it is thick enough to retain a slight peak briefly when beater or whisk is withdrawn (3 to 6 minutes).

3. Working quickly, pour warm egg mixture into a large bowl. Fold in about a third of the whipped topping to lighten egg mixture; then fold in remaining whipped topping. Serve immediately.

4. To serve, lift fruit from pan with a slotted spoon and divide among six 8-ounce (240-ml) stemmed glasses; discard cooking liquid or reserve for other uses. Top with zabaglione cream. Makes 6 servings.

Per serving: 346 calories (22% calories from fat), 8 g total fat, 4 g saturated fat, 213 mg cholesterol, 24 mg sodium, 61 g carbohydrates, 3 g fiber, 4 g protein, 48 mg calcium, 2 mg iron

Thin fennel slices add a licorice-flavored surprise to this unusual apple tart.

- ½ cup (75 g) dried currants
- ¾ cup plus 2 teaspoons (100 g) all-purpose flour
- ½ cup (40 g) regular rolled oats
- ¼ cup (55 g) butter or margarine, cut into chunks
- 1 large egg white
- ⅓ cup (70 g) granulated sugar
- 1 teaspoon ground cinnamon
- 2 cups (220 g) sliced apples such as Newtown Pippin (cut slices ¼ inch/6 mm thick)
- 1½ cups (148 g) sliced fennel (cut slices ¼ inch/6 mm thick)
- 2 teaspoons lemon juice
  About 2 tablespoons sifted powdered sugar

Apple-Fennel Tart

Preparation time: 30 minutes
Cooking time: About 1¼ hours
Pictured on facing page

1. Place currants in a small bowl and add enough water to cover. Let stand until currants are softened (about 10 minutes), stirring occasionally. Drain well; set aside.

2. In a food processor, combine ¾ cup (95 g) of the flour, oats, and butter. Whirl until mixture resembles fine crumbs. Add egg white; whirl until dough holds together. Press dough evenly over bottom and sides of an 8-inch (20-cm) tart pan with a removable rim.

3. In a large bowl, mix remaining 2 teaspoons flour, granulated sugar, cinnamon, and currants. Add apples, fennel, and lemon juice; mix well. Pour fruit mixture into pan; pat to make level.

4. Bake on lowest rack of a 425°F (220°C) oven until top of filling begins to brown (about 45 minutes). Drape tart with foil; continue to bake until juices begin to bubble (about 30 more minutes).

5. Remove pan rim; slide a wide spatula under hot tart to release crust (leave tart in place). Serve warm or cool; dust with powdered sugar before serving. Makes 6 servings.

Per serving: 268 calories (27% calories from fat), 8 g total fat, 5 g saturated fat, 21 mg cholesterol, 116 mg sodium, 46 g carbohydrates, 3 g fiber, 4 g protein, 38 mg calcium, 2 mg iron

---

A cross between candy and fruitcake, panforte ("strong bread") is loaded with fruits and nuts.

- 1 cup (130 g) salted roasted almonds, coarsely chopped
- 1 cup (about 5 oz./140 g) dried pitted tart cherries
- 1 cup (185 g) *each* candied orange peel and candied lemon peel, finely chopped
- 1 teaspoon *each* grated lemon peel and ground cinnamon
- ½ teaspoon ground coriander
- ¼ teaspoon *each* ground cloves and ground nutmeg
- ½ cup (60 g) all-purpose flour
- ¾ cup (150 g) granulated sugar
- ¾ cup (180 ml) honey
- 2 tablespoons butter or margarine
- ½ cup (50 g) sifted powdered sugar

Panforte

Preparation time: 25 minutes
Cooking time: About 1¼ hours

1. In a large bowl, combine almonds, cherries, candied orange peel, candied lemon peel, grated lemon peel, cinnamon, coriander, cloves, nutmeg, and flour. Mix until nuts and fruit pieces are thoroughly coated with flour; set aside.

2. In a deep medium-size pan, combine granulated sugar, honey, and butter. Cook over high heat, stirring often, until mixture registers 265°F/129°C (hard-ball stage) on a candy thermometer. Working quickly, pour hot syrup over fruit mixture and mix thoroughly. Immediately scrape mixture into a

heavily greased, floured 8- to 9-inch (20- to 23-cm) cake pan.

3. Bake in a 300°F (150°C) oven for 1 hour; if cake begins to brown excessively, drape it loosely with foil (don't let foil touch cake). Let cool completely in pan on a rack.

4. Sprinkle a work surface with half the powdered sugar. Using a slender knife and spatula, loosen sides and bottom of cake from pan, then invert cake (prying gently, if needed) onto sugared surface. Sprinkle and pat sugar over entire cake. Then dust cake with remaining powdered sugar to coat completely. Transfer to a platter. To serve, cut into wedges. Makes 12 servings.

Per serving: 370 calories (24% calories from fat), 10 g total fat, 2 g saturated fat, 5 mg cholesterol, 131 mg sodium, 71 g carbohydrates, 2 g fiber, 4 g protein, 37 mg calcium, 0.9 mg iron

Apple-Fennel Tart
(recipe on facing page)

Espresso Chocolate Cake with Orange Sauce

Preparation time: 35 minutes
Cooking time: 35 to 40 minutes
Pictured on page 94

2 tablespoons butter or margarine, at room temperature

1 cup (220 g) firmly packed brown sugar

1 large egg

3 large egg whites

1 cup (240 ml) nonfat sour cream

1 teaspoon vanilla

¾ cup (95 g) all-purpose flour

⅓ cup (29 g) unsweetened cocoa powder

1 tablespoon instant espresso powder

1½ teaspoons baking powder

6 or 7 large oranges (about 8 oz./230 g *each*)

6 tablespoons (72 g) granulated sugar

4 teaspoons cornstarch

1½ teaspoons instant espresso powder (or to taste)

1½ cups (360 ml) fresh orange juice

2 tablespoons (30 ml) orange-flavored liqueur (or to taste)

2 tablespoons unsweetened cocoa powder

Mint sprigs

1. In a food processor or a large bowl, combine butter and brown sugar; whirl or beat with an electric mixer until well blended. Add egg, egg whites, sour cream, and vanilla; whirl or beat until well blended. Add flour, the ⅓ cup (29 g) cocoa, the 1 tablespoon instant espresso, and baking powder; whirl or beat just until combined. Spread batter in a greased 8-inch-square (20-cm-square) nonstick or regular baking pan. Bake in a 350°F (175°C) oven until cake begins to pull away from pan sides and center springs back when lightly pressed (35 to 40 minutes).

2. While cake is baking, finely shred enough peel (colored part only) from oranges to make 1 to 2 teaspoons for sauce; cover and set aside. Cut off and discard remaining peel and all white membrane from oranges. Cut between membranes to release segments. Cover orange segments and set aside.

3. In a small pan, combine granulated sugar, cornstarch, and the 1½ teaspoons instant espresso. Whisk in orange juice and the reserved shredded orange peel; cook over medium-high heat, stirring constantly, until sauce boils and thickens slightly (about 1 minute). Remove from heat and stir in liqueur.

4. Just before serving, sift the 2 tablespoons cocoa over cake. Cut cake into diamonds, triangles, or squares; transfer to individual plates. Arrange orange segments alongside. Drizzle sauce over oranges. Garnish with mint sprigs. Makes 8 servings.

Per serving: 361 calories (12% calories from fat), 5 g total fat, 2 g saturated fat, 34 mg cholesterol, 187 mg sodium, 74 g carbohydrates, 5 g fiber, 8 g protein, 189 mg calcium, 2 mg iron

Espresso Biscotti

Preparation time: 35 minutes
Cooking time: About 35 minutes
Pictured on page 94

½ cup (68 g) hazelnuts

5 tablespoons (71 g) butter or margarine, at room temperature

½ cup (100 g) granulated sugar

2½ teaspoons instant espresso powder

1 large egg

2 large egg whites

1 teaspoon vanilla

2 cups (250 g) all-purpose flour

2 teaspoons baking powder

1½ cups (150 g) sifted powdered sugar

1. Spread hazelnuts in a single layer in a shallow baking pan. Bake in a 375°F (190°C) oven until nuts are golden beneath skins (about 10 minutes). Let nuts cool slightly; then pour into a towel, fold to enclose, and rub to remove as much of loose skins as possible. Let cool; chop coarsely and set aside. Reduce oven temperature to 350°F (175°C).

2. In a large bowl, beat butter, granulated sugar, and 1½ teaspoons of the instant espresso until well blended. Add egg and egg whites, beating until well blended. Stir in vanilla. In a medium-size bowl, stir together flour and baking powder; add to butter mixture and stir until well blended. Mix in hazelnuts.

3. Divide dough in half. On a lightly floured board, shape each portion into a long roll about 1½ inches (3.5 cm) in diameter. Place rolls on a large nonstick or greased regular baking sheet, spacing them 3 inches (8 cm) apart. Flatten rolls to make ½-inch-thick (1-cm-thick) loaves. Bake in a 350°F (175°C) oven until loaves feel firm to the touch (about 15 minutes).

4. Remove baking sheet from oven and let loaves

cool for 3 to 5 minutes; then cut crosswise into slices about ½ inch (1 cm) thick. Tip slices cut side down on baking sheet (at this point, you may need another sheet to bake biscotti all at once). Return to oven and continue to bake until biscotti look dry and are lightly browned (about 10 minutes); if using 2 baking sheets, switch their positions halfway through baking. Transfer biscotti to racks and let cool.

5. Meanwhile, in a small bowl, dissolve remaining 1 teaspoon instant espresso in 4 teaspoons (20 ml) very hot water. Stir in powdered sugar; if needed, add more hot water, 1 teaspoon at a time, to make icing easy to spread.

6. Spread icing over 1 to 1½ inches (2.5 to 3.5 cm) of one end of each cooled cookie. Let stand until icing is firm before serving. Makes about 4 dozen cookies.

Per cookie: 60 calories (30% calories from fat), 2 g total fat, 0.7 g saturated fat, 7 mg cholesterol, 35 mg sodium, 10 g carbohydrates, 0.2 g fiber, 1 g protein, 15 mg calcium, 0.3 mg iron

Chocolate-Espresso Sauce

Preparation time: 10 minutes
Cooking time: About 5 minutes

½ cup (110 g) firmly packed brown sugar

¼ cup (22 g) unsweetened cocoa powder

4 teaspoons cornstarch

1 teaspoon instant espresso powder

2 tablespoons (30 ml) light corn syrup

1 teaspoon coffee-flavored liqueur

½ teaspoon vanilla

1. In a small pan, mix sugar, cocoa, cornstarch, and instant espresso. Add corn syrup and ½ cup (120 ml) water; stir until smooth. Cook over medium-high heat, stirring constantly and scraping sides of pan often, until sauce comes to a rapid boil and thickens slightly (about 5 minutes).

2. Remove pan from heat and stir in liqueur and vanilla. Serve warm; just before serving, stir well. If made ahead, let cool; then cover and refrigerate for up to 1 week. Before serving, bring to a gentle boil over medium-low heat, stirring often. Makes about 1 cup (240 ml).

Per tablespoon: 40 calories (4% calories from fat), 0.2 g total fat, 0.1 g saturated fat, 0 mg cholesterol, 6 mg sodium, 10 g carbohydrates, 0.4 g fiber, 0.3 g protein, 8 mg calcium, 0.3 mg iron

Espresso Cheesecake

Preparation time: 25 minutes
Cooking time: 1½ to 1¾ hours
Cooling & chilling time:
At least 4½ hours
Pictured on page 94

1 package (about 9 oz./ 255 g) chocolate wafer cookies

¼ cup (55 g) butter or margarine, melted and cooled slightly

1 tablespoon instant espresso powder

½ teaspoon vanilla

4 large packages (about 8 oz./230 g *each*) nonfat cream cheese, at room temperature

1 cup (200 g) sugar

3 large eggs

2 large egg whites

2 cups (470 ml) nonfat sour cream

3 tablespoons (45 ml) coffee-flavored liqueur

1 tablespoon sugar

1 tablespoon unsweetened cocoa powder

Chocolate-covered espresso beans or mocha candy beans

1. In a food processor, whirl cookies to form fine crumbs. Add butter, instant espresso, and vanilla; whirl just until crumbs are evenly moistened. Press crumb mixture firmly over bottom and about 1 inch (2.5 cm) up sides of a greased 9-inch (23-cm) cheesecake pan with a removable

rim. Bake in a 350°F (175°C) oven until crust feels slightly firmer when pressed (about 15 minutes).

2. In clean food processor or in a large bowl, combine cream cheese, the 1 cup (200 g) sugar, eggs, egg whites, 1 cup (240 ml) of the sour cream, and liqueur. Whirl or beat with an electric mixer until smooth.

3. Pour cheese filling into baked crust. Return to oven and bake until filling is golden on top and jiggles only slightly in center when pan is gently shaken (1¼ to 1½ hours).

4. Gently run a slender knife between cheesecake and pan rim; then let cheesecake cool in pan on a rack for 30 minutes. Meanwhile, in a small bowl, gently stir together remaining 1 cup (240 ml) sour cream and the 1 tablespoon sugar; cover and refrigerate.

5. Spread cooled cheesecake with sour cream topping. Cover and refrigerate until cold (at least 4 hours) or until next day. Just before serving, sprinkle with cocoa; then remove pan rim. Garnish with chocolate-covered espresso beans. Makes 12 to 16 servings.

Per serving: 276 calories (23% calories from fat), 7 g total fat, 3 g saturated fat, 62 mg cholesterol, 492 mg sodium, 37 g carbohydrates, 0.7 g fiber, 15 g protein, 239 mg calcium, 0.9 mg iron

Espresso Cheesecake, Espresso Biscotti, and Espresso
Chocolate Cake with Orange Sauce
(recipes on pages 92–93)

Index